URBAN LAND INSTITUTE

Award Winning Projects 2006

Deloitte.

This book was made possible in part through the generous sponsorship of Deloitte & Touche USA LLP.

URBAN LAND INSTITUTE
AWARD WINNING PROJECTS 2006

Julie Stern and David Takesuye

ULI–the Urban Land Institute
1025 Thomas Jefferson Street, N.W.
Suite 500 West
Washington, D.C. 20007-5201

Library of Congress Cataloging-in-Publication Data

Stern, Julie D.
   Urban Land Institute award winning projects 2006 / Julie Stern and David Takesuye.
      p. cm.
   ISBN-13: 978-0-87420-970-9 (alk. paper)
      1. Land use, Urban. I. Takesuye, David. II. Urban Land Institute.
   III. Title.
   HD1391.S74 2006
   333.77–dc22   2006025721

ISBN: 978-0-87420-970-9

10 9 8 7 6 5 4 3 2 1

Printed and bound in Canada

Design and composition
Marc Alain Meadows, Meadows Design Office Inc., Washington, D.C.
www.mdomedia.com

ULI–the Urban Land Institute is a nonprofit education and research institute that is supported by its members. Its mission is to provide responsible leadership in the use of land in order to enhance the total environment.

ULI sponsors education programs and forums to encourage an open international exchange of ideas and sharing of experiences; initiates research that anticipates emerging land use trends and issues and proposes creative solutions based on that research; provides advisory services; and publishes a wide variety of materials to disseminate information on land use and development. Established in 1936, the Institute today has more than 32,000 members from over 80 countries, representing the entire spectrum of the land use and development disciplines. The Institute is recognized throughout the world as one of America's most respected and widely quoted sources of objective information on urban planning, growth, and development.

Project Staff

Rachelle L. Levitt
Executive Vice President, Information Group
Publisher

Dean Schwanke
Senior Vice President, Publications and Awards

Jo Allen Gause
Senior Director, Residential Development

David Takesuye
Senior Associate, Awards and Competitions
Project Director

Nancy H. Stewart
Director, Book Program
Managing Editor

Lori Hatcher
Director, Publications Marketing

Duke Johns
Manuscript Editor

Betsy VanBuskirk
Art Director

Karrie Underwood
Digital Images Assistant

Craig Chapman
Director, Publishing Operations

Avery Salisbury
Research Intern

The ULI Awards for Excellence Program

A guiding principle of the Urban Land Institute is that the achievement of excellence in land use practice should be recognized and rewarded. Since 1979, ULI has honored outstanding development projects in both the private and public sectors with the ULI Awards for Excellence program, which today is widely recognized as the development community's most prestigious awards program. ULI Awards for Excellence recognize the full development process of a project, not just its architecture or design—although these elements play an important role in the overall project. Each award is presented to the development project, with the developer accepting on behalf of the project.

Nominations are open to all, not just ULI members. Finalists and winners are chosen by juries of ULI full members chaired by trustees. Jury members represent many fields of real estate development expertise, including finance, land planning, development, public affairs, design, and other professional services. They also represent a broad geographic diversity.

ULI began the Awards for Excellence program in 1979 with the objective of recognizing truly superior development efforts. The criteria for the awards involve factors that go beyond good design, including leadership, contribution to the community, innovations, public/private partnership, environmental protection and enhancement, response to societal needs, and financial success. Winning projects represent the highest standards of achievement in the development industry, standards that ULI members hold worthy of attainment in their professional endeavors. All types of projects have been recognized for their excellence, including office, residential, recreational, urban/mixed use, industrial/office park, commercial/retail, new community, rehabilitation, public, and heritage projects, as well as programs and projects that do not fit into any of these product categories.

For the first three years of the program, only one Award for Excellence was granted each year. In 1982, ULI trustees authorized awards for two winners—one large-scale project and one small-scale project—to recognize excellence regardless of size. Starting in 1985, the awards program shifted emphasis to product categories, while also retaining the small- and large-scale designations. As the program matured, new categories were added to reflect changes in the development industry. In 2002, the last year in which winners were awarded by category, there were 18 categories and up to 11 possible awards.

The Special Award was established in 1986 to acknowledge up to two projects and/or programs that are socially desirable but do not necessarily meet the official awards guidelines governing financial viability, and exemplary projects that are not easily categorized. In 1989, the Heritage Award was introduced to acknowledge projects that have established an industry standard for excellence, and that have been completed for at least 25 years. As of 2006, only seven Heritage Awards have been granted.

When the awards program began, only projects located in the United States or Canada were considered. Beginning with the 1994 awards, ULI's board of trustees authorized the creation of an International Award for a project outside the United States and Canada. With the 2001 awards, the board eliminated this category, opening all categories to all projects, regardless of location.

In 2003, ULI eliminated all category designations, with the exception of the Heritage Award, and did more to recognize the excellence of all the finalist projects in the awards process, not just the award winners. In 2004, ULI inaugurated the ULI Awards for Excellence: Europe, adopting the same criteria and a similar selection process, and juried by Europe-based ULI members. And in 2005, the Awards for Excellence program continued to evolve with the introduction of the ULI Awards for Excellence: Asia Pacific. Building on the success of the Europe awards, the Asia Pacific awards program selected five winners in 2005.

Also new in 2005 was the introduction of the ULI Global Awards for Excellence. A select jury of international members, charged with choosing up to five Global Award winners from among last year's 21 award-winning projects, announced three Global Award winners (see pages 136–137) at the Institute's 2005 Fall Meeting in Los Angeles, November 4, 2005. Again, in 2006, up to five Global Award winners among the 20 winners profiled in this book will be announced at the 2006 Fall Meeting in Denver, October 20, 2006.

The 2007 "Call for Entries" for the Americas, Europe, and Asia Pacific competitions is now available on the ULI Awards Web page (www.awards.uli.org).

Judging Criteria

1. Although architectural excellence is certainly a factor, the ULI Awards for Excellence is not a "beauty contest."

2. The project or program must be substantially completed. If the project is phased, the first phase must be completed and operationally stable.

3. No specific age or time constraints apply, except for the Heritage Award (which recognizes projects and/or programs that have been completed for at least 25 years).

4. The project must be financially viable, which means it must be in stable operation and financially successful. An applicant must be able to document the prudent use of financial resources to justify the achievement of a financial return. Programs and projects developed by nonprofit or public agencies are necessarily exempt from the financial viability requirement.

5. The project must demonstrate relevance to the contemporary and future needs of the community in which it is located. The community reaction to the project also is taken into consideration.

6. The project must stand out from others in its category.

7. The project must be an exemplary representative of good development and a model for similar projects worldwide.

Selection Process

1. Applications are solicited via a "Call for Entries," available as a downloadable document on the ULI Web site's Awards page (www.awards.uli.org) on October 1.

2. Developers and/or other members of the development team submit completed applications to ULI by a given date in January. Each completed entry must contain the developer's name and signature.

3. The three Awards for Excellence juries—the Americas, Europe, and Asia Pacific—separately convene to review submissions and choose finalists.

4. Teams of two or three jury members visit each finalist project.

5. When all site visits have been completed, the respective juries reconvene to evaluate the finalist projects and choose award winners—up to ten in the Americas, five in Europe, and five in Asia Pacific. In the Americas, the jury may also choose one Heritage Award winner.

The Americas awards are announced and officially honored at an awards ceremony at ULI's annual Spring Council Forum. The Europe and Asia Pacific awards are announced at their respective spring or summer conferences.

Past ULI Awards for Excellence Winners

The following 206 projects have received ULI Awards for Excellence. Each project name is followed by its location and its developer/owner.

1979 *First year of award* ▪ The Galleria; Houston, Texas; Hines Interests Limited Partnership

1980 Charles Center; Baltimore, Maryland; Baltimore City Development Corporation

1981 WDW/Reedy Creek; Orlando, Florida; The Walt Disney Company

1982 *Two awards given: large- and small-scale* ▪ Large-Scale: Heritage Village; Southbury, Connecticut; Heritage Development Group, Inc. ▪ Small-Scale: Promontory Point; Newport Beach, California; The Irvine Company

1983 Large-Scale: Eaton Centre; Toronto, Canada; Cadillac Fairview Limited

1984 Large-Scale: Embarcadero Center; San Francisco, California; Embarcadero Center, Ltd.; ▪ Small-Scale: Rainbow Centre; Niagara Falls, New York; The Cordish Company

1985 *Introduction of product categories* ▪ New Community: Las Colinas; Irving, Texas; JPI Partners, Inc. ▪ Large-Scale Residential: Museum Tower; New York, New York; The Charles H. Shaw Company ▪ Small-Scale Urban Mixed-Use: Sea Colony Condominiums; Santa Monica, California; Dominion Property Company ▪ Large-Scale Recreational: Sea Pines Plantation; Hilton Head, South Carolina; Community Development Institute ▪ Small-Scale Urban Mixed-Use: Vista Montoya; Los Angeles, California; Pico Union Neighborhood Council/Community Redevelopment Agency

1986 *Introduction of rehabilitation and special categories* ▪ Small-Scale Mixed-Use: 2000 Pennsylvania Avenue; Washington, D.C.; George Washington University ▪ Small-Scale Rehabilitation: Downtown Costa Mesa; Costa Mesa, California; PSB Realty Corporation ▪ Special: Inner Harbor Shoreline; Baltimore, Maryland; Baltimore City Development Corporation ▪ Large-Scale Recreational: Kaanapali Beach Resort; Kaanapali, Hawaii; Amfac/JMB Hawaii ▪ Large-Scale Residential: The Landings on Skidaway Island; Savannah, Georgia; The Bramigar Organization, Inc. ▪ Small-Scale Industrial/Office Park: The Purdue Frederick Company; Norwalk, Connecticut; The Purdue Frederick Company ▪ Large-Scale Recreational: Water Tower Place; Chicago, Illinois; JMB Realty Corporation

1987 Large-Scale Industrial/Office Park: Bishop Ranch Business Park; San Ramon, California; Sunset Development Company ▪ Small-Scale Commercial/Retail: Loews Ventana Canyon Resort; Tucson, Arizona; Estes Homebuilding ▪ Large-Scale Urban Mixed-Use: St. Louis Union Station; St. Louis, Missouri; The Rouse Company ▪ Small-Scale Residential: Straw Hill; Manchester, New Hampshire; George Matarazzo and Mark Stebbins ▪ Rehabilitation: The Willard Inter-Continental; Washington, D.C.; The Oliver Carr Company

1988 Large-Scale Urban Mixed-Use: Copley Place; Boston, Massachusetts; Urban Investment & Development Company ▪ Special: Downtown Women's Center; Los Angeles, California; The Ratkovitch Company ▪ Large-Scale Commercial/Retail: The Grand Avenue; Milwaukee, Wisconsin; Milwaukee Redevelopment Corporation (MRC) ▪ Rehabilitation: Northpoint; Chicago, Illinois; Amoco Neighborhood Development ▪ Small-Scale Residential: Pickleweed Apartments; Mill Valley, California; BRIDGE Housing Corporation ▪ Large-Scale Residential: Rector Place; New York, New York; Battery Park City Authority ▪ Small-Scale Office: Wilshire Palisades; Santa Monica, California; Tooley & Company

1989 *Introduction of Heritage Award* ▪ Small-Scale Urban Mixed-Use: Charleston Place; Charleston, South Carolina; The Taubman Company, Inc., and Cordish Embry Associates (joint venture) ▪ Rehabilitation: Commonwealth Development; Boston, Massachusetts; Corcoran Management ▪ Small-Scale Office: Escondido City Hall; Escondido, California; City of Escondido ▪ Large-Scale Office: Norwest Center; Minneapolis, Minnesota; Hines Interests ▪ Special: Pratt-Willert Neighborhood; Buffalo, New York; City of Buffalo ▪ New Community: Reston; Reston, Virginia; Mobil Land Development in Virginia ▪ Heritage Award: Rockefeller Center; New York, New York; The Rockefeller Group ▪ Large-Scale Urban Mixed-Use: Rowes Wharf; Boston, Massachusetts; The Beacon Companies

1990 Small-Scale Commercial: The Boulders; Carefree, Arizona; Westcor Partners ▪ Large-Scale Industrial: Carnegie Center; Princeton, New Jersey; Carnegie Center Associates ▪ Small-Scale Residential: Columbia Place; San Diego, California; Odmark & Thelan ▪ Large-Scale Residential: River Run; Boise, Idaho; O'Neill Enterprises, Inc. ▪ Special: Tent City; Boston, Massachusetts; Tent City Corporation ▪ Rehabilitation: Wayne County Building; Detroit, Michigan; Farbman Stein ▪ New Community: Woodlake; Richmond, Virginia; East West Partners of Virginia

1991 Small-Scale Commercial/Retail: Del Mar Plaza; Del Mar, California; Del Mar Partnership ▪ Large-Scale Urban Mixed-Use: Fashion Centre at Pentagon City; Arlington, Virginia; Melvin Simon & Associates, and Rose Associates ▪ Small-Scale Urban Mixed-Use: Garibaldi Square; Chicago, Illinois; The Charles H. Shaw Company ▪ Large-Scale Residential: Ghent Square; Norfolk, Virginia; Norfolk Redevelopment and Housing Authority ▪ Special: Grand Central Partnership; New York, New York; Grand Central Partnership ▪ Small-Scale Office: James R. Mills Building; San Diego, California; Starboard Development Corporation ▪ Rehabilitation: Marina Village; Alameda, California; Vintage Properties ▪ Special: Union Station; Washington, D.C.; Union Station Redevelopment Corporation

1992 Small-Scale Commercial/Retail: CocoWalk; Miami, Florida; Constructa U.S. ▪ Special: The Coeur d'Alene Resort Golf Course; Coeur d'Alene, Idaho; Hagadone Hospitality ▪ Special: The Delancey Street Foundation; San Francisco, California; The Delancey Street Foundation ▪ Public: Harbor Point; Boston, Massachusetts; Corcoran Jennison Companies ▪ Large-Scale Mixed-Use: Market Square; Washington, D.C.; Trammell Crow ▪ New Community: Planned Community of Mission Viejo; Mission Viejo, California; Mission Viejo Company ▪ Small-Scale Residential: Summit Place; St. Paul, Minnesota; Robert Engstrom Companies ▪ Rehabilitation: Tysons Corner Center; McLean, Virginia; The L&B Group

1993 Small-Scale Residential: Beverly Hills Senior Housing; Beverly Hills, California; Jewish Federation Council ▪ Special: Charlestown Navy Yard; Charlestown, Massachusetts; Boston Redevelopment Authority ▪ Heritage Award: The Country Club Plaza; Kansas City, Missouri; J.C. Nichols Company ▪ Large-Scale Residential: The Cypress of Hilton Head Island; Hilton Head Island, South Carolina; The Melrose Company ▪ Small-Scale Rehabilitation: Furness House; Baltimore, Maryland; The Cordish Company ▪ Large-Scale Recreational: Kapalua; Kapalua, Maui, Hawaii; Kapalua Land Company, Ltd. ▪ Special: Post Office Square Park and Garage; Boston, Massachusetts; Friends of Post Office Square, Inc. ▪ Rehabilitation: Schlitz Park; Milwaukee, Wisconsin; The Brewery Works, Inc. ▪ Small-Scale Commercial/Retail: The Somerset Collection; Troy, Michigan; Forbes/Cohen Properties and Frankel Associates

1994 *Introduction of international category* ▪ International: Broadgate; London, United Kingdom; Stanhope Properties ▪ Small-Scale Residential: Orchard Village; Chattanooga, Tennessee; Chattanooga Neighborhood Enterprise ▪ Public: Oriole Park at Camden Yards; Baltimore, Maryland; Maryland Stadium Authority ▪ Special: The Pennsylvania Avenue Plan; Washington, D.C.; Pennsylvania Avenue Development Corporation ▪ Large-Scale Rehabilitation: Phipps Plaza; Atlanta, Georgia; Compass Retail, Inc. ▪ Heritage Award: Sea Pines Plantation; Hilton Head Island, South Carolina; Charles Fraser ▪ Large-Scale Office: Washington Mutual Tower; Seattle, Washington; Wright Runstad and Company ▪ Large-Scale Residential: Woodbridge; Irvine, California; The Irvine Company ▪ Special: The Woodlands; The Woodlands, Texas; The Woodlands Corporation

1995 Small-Scale Rehabilitation: 640 Memorial Drive; Cambridge, Massachusetts; Massachusetts Institute of Technology Real Estate ▪ Large-Scale Commercial/Retail: Broadway Plaza; Walnut Creek, California; Macerich Northwestern Associates and The Macerich Company ▪ Heritage Award: Disneyland Park; Anaheim, California; The Walt Disney Company ▪ Large-Scale Industrial/Office: Irvine Spectrum; Orange County, California; The Irvine Company ▪ Small-Scale Recreational: Little Nell Hotel and Aspen Mountain Base; Aspen, Colorado; Aspen Skiing Company ▪ Special: Monterey Bay Aquarium; Monterey, California; The Monterey Bay Aquarium Foundation ▪ New Community: Pelican Bay; Naples, Florida; WCI Communities, LP ▪ Special: Riverbank State Park; New York, New York; New York State Office of Parks, Recreation and Historic Preservation ▪ Small-Scale Residential: Strathern Park Apartments; Sun Valley, California; Thomas Safran and Associates

1996 Large-Scale Residential: Avenel; Potomac, Maryland; Natelli Communities ▪ Public: Bryant Park; New York, New York; Bryant Park Restoration Corporation ▪ Large-Scale Office: Comerica Tower at Detroit Center; Detroit, Michigan; Hines Interests Limited Partnership ▪ Small-Scale Residential: The Court Home Collection at Valencia NorthPark; Valencia, California; The Newhall Land and Farming Company, and RGC ▪ Small-Scale Commercial/Hotel: The Forum Shops; Las Vegas, Nevada; Simon Property Group ▪ Small-Scale Mixed-Use: The Heritage on the Garden; Boston, Massachusetts; The Druker Company ▪ Large-Scale Recreational:

Kiawah Island; Kiawah Island, South Carolina; Kiawah Resort Associates LP ▪ Special: The Scattered Site Program; Chicago, Illinois; The Habitat Company

1997 Heritage Award: The Arizona Biltmore Hotel and Resort; Phoenix, Arizona; Grossman Company Properties ▪ Rehabilitation: Chelsea Piers; New York, New York; Chelsea Piers, LP ▪ Large-Scale Recreational: Desert Mountain; Scottsdale, Arizona; Desert Mountain Properties ▪ Rehabilitation: Eagles Building Restoration; Seattle, Washington; A Contemporary Theater and Housing Resources Group (general partners) ▪ Small-Scale Residential: Mercado Apartments; San Diego, California; City of San Diego Redevelopment Agency ▪ Large-Scale Commercial/Hotel: Park Meadows; Park Meadows, Colorado; TrizecHahn Centers ▪ Special: Pennsylvania Convention Center; Philadelphia, Pennsylvania; Pennsylvania Convention Center Authority ▪ Special: A Safe House for Kids and Moms; Irvine, California; Human Options ▪ Public: Smyrna Town Center; Smyrna, Georgia; City of Smyrna, Knight-Davidson Companies (residential) and Thomas Enterprises (retail/offices) ▪ International: Stockley Park at Heathrow; Uxbridge, Middlesex, United Kingdom; Stanhope Properties, PLC

1998 Large-Scale Business Park: Alliance; Fort Worth, Texas; Hillwood Development Corporation ▪ Special: American Visionary Art Museum; Baltimore, Maryland; Rebecca and LeRoy E. Hoffberger ▪ International: Calakmul; Mexico City, Mexico; Francisco G. Coronado (owner) ▪ Small-Scale Residential: Courthouse Hill; Arlington, Virginia; Eakin/Youngentob Associates, Inc. ▪ Public: Harold Washington Library Center; Chicago, Illinois; U.S. Equities Realty (developer) ▪ Special: Richmond City Center; Richmond, California; BRIDGE Housing Corporation (owner) ▪ Rehabilitation: Twenty-Eight State Street; Boston, Massachusetts; Equity Office Properties Trust ▪ Rehabilitation: UtiliCorp United World Headquarters/New York Life Building; Kansas City, Missouri; The Zimmer Companies ▪ Small-Scale Recreational: Village Center; Beaver Creek, Colorado; East West Partners

1999 Small-Scale Rehabilitation: Bayou Place; Houston, Texas; The Cordish Company ▪ Large-Scale Residential: Bonita Bay; Bonita Springs, Florida; Bonita Bay Properties, Inc. ▪ Public: Chicago Public Schools Capital Improvement Program; Chicago, Illinois; Chicago Public Schools ▪ Small-Scale Commercial/Hotel: The Commons at Calabasas; Calabasas, California; Caruso Affiliated Holdings ▪ Special: Coors Field; Denver, Colorado; Denver Metropolitan Stadium District ▪ Small-Scale Mixed-Use: East Pointe; Milwaukee, Wisconsin; Milwaukee Redevelopment Corporation and Mandel Group, Inc. ▪ Large-Scale Recreational: Hualalai; Ka'upulehu-Kona, Hawaii; Ka'upulehu Makai Venture/Hualalai Development Company ▪ Large-Scale Rehabilitation: John Hancock Center; Chicago, Illinois; U.S. Equities Realty ▪ Small-Scale Residential: Normandie Village; Los Angeles, California; O.N.E. Company, SIPA ▪ Small-Scale Commercial/Hotel: Seventh & Collins Parking Facility (Ballet Valet); Miami Beach, Florida; City of Miami Beach, Goldman Properties ▪ International: Vinohradský Pavilon; Prague, Czech Republic; Prague Investment, a.s.

2000 Small-Scale Rehabilitation: Amazon.com Building; Seattle, Washington; Wright Runstad and Company ▪ Heritage Award: The Burnham Plan; Chicago, Illinois; The Commercial Club of Chicago ▪ Small-Scale Residential: The Colony; Newport Beach, California; Irvine Apartment Communities ▪ Large-Scale Residential: Coto de Caza; Orange County, California; Lennar Communities ▪ Small-Scale Mixed-Use: DePaul Center; Chicago, Illinois; DePaul University ▪ Public: NorthLake Park Community School; Orlando, Florida; Lake Nona Land Company ▪ Large-Scale Rehabilitation: The Power Plant; Baltimore, Maryland; The Cordish Company ▪ International: Sony Center am Potsdamer Platz; Berlin, Germany; Tishman Speyer Properties, Sony Corporation, Kajima Corporation, and BE-ST Development GmbH & Co. (owner) ▪ Special:

Spring Island; Beaufort County, South Carolina; Chaffin/Light Associates ▪ Public: The Townhomes on Capitol Hill; Washington, D.C.; Ellen Wilson CDC and Telesis Corporation ▪ Large-Scale Recreational: Whistler Village/Blackcomb Benchlands; Whistler, British Columbia, Canada; Resort Municipality of Whistler, and INTRAWEST Corporation

2001 *International category eliminated* ▪ New Community: Celebration; Celebration, Florida; The Celebration Company ▪ Special: Dewees Island; Dewees Island, South Carolina; Island Preservation Partnership ▪ Large-Scale Residential: Harbor Steps; Seattle, Washington; Harbor Properties, Inc. ▪ Small-Scale Rehabilitation: Pier 1; San Francisco, California; AMB Property Corporation ▪ Small-Scale Recreational: The Reserve; Indian Wells, California; Lowe Enterprises, Inc. ▪ Small-Scale Office: Thames Court; London, United Kingdom; Markborough Properties Limited ▪ Special: Townhomes at Oxon Creek; Washington, D.C.; William C. Smith & Company, Inc. ▪ Large-Scale Mixed-Use: Valencia Town Center Drive; Valencia, California; The Newhall Land and Farming Company ▪ Large-Scale Commercial/Hotel: The Venetian Casino Resort; Las Vegas, Nevada; LVS/Development Group ▪ Public: Yerba Buena Gardens; San Francisco, California; Yerba Buena Alliance

2002 Small-Scale Mixed-Use: Bethesda Row; Bethesda, Maryland; Federal Realty Investment Trust ▪ Large-Scale Mixed-Use: CityPlace; West Palm Beach, Florida; The Related Companies ▪ Special: Envision Utah; Salt Lake City, Utah; Coalition for Utah's Future ▪ Public: Homan Square Community Center Campus; Chicago, Illinois; Homan Square Community Center Foundation (owner) and The Shaw Company (developer) ▪ Small-Scale Rehabilitation: Hotel Burnham at the Reliance Building; Chicago, Illinois; McCaffery Interests ▪ Special: Memphis Ballpark District; Memphis, Tennessee; Memphis Redbirds Foundation (owner), and Parkway Properties, Inc. (developer) ▪ Large-Scale Office: One Raffles Link; Singapore Central, Singapore; Hongkong Land Property Co., Ltd. ▪ Small-Scale Rehabilitation: REI Denver Flagship Store; Denver, Colorado; Recreational Equipment, Inc. ▪ Large-Scale Recreational: Station Mont Tremblant; Quebec, Canada; Intrawest ▪ New Community: Summerlin North; Las Vegas, Nevada; The Rouse Company

2003 *Product categories eliminated* ▪ Atago Green Hills; Tokyo, Japan; Mori Building Company ▪ Ayala Center Greenbelt 3; Makati City, Manila, Philippines; Ayala Land, Inc. ▪ Bay Harbor; Bay Harbor, Michigan; Victor International Corporation ▪ Chattahoochee River Greenway; Georgia; Chattahoochee River Coordinating Committee ▪ The Grove and Farmers Market; Los Angeles, California; Caruso Affiliated Holdings (The Grove), and A.F. Gilmore Company (Farmers Market) ▪ Millennium Place; Boston, Massachusetts; Millennium Partners/MDA Associates ▪ Shanghai Xintiandi (North Block); Shanghai, China; Shui On Group ▪ The Town of Seaside; Seaside, Florida; Seaside Community Development Corporation ▪ The Villages of East Lake; Atlanta, Georgia; East Lake Community Foundation, Inc. ▪ The West Philadelphia Initiatives; Philadelphia, Pennsylvania; University of Pennsylvania

2004 The Americas and Asia Pacific: Baldwin Park; Orlando, Florida; Baldwin Park Development Company ▪ Fall Creek Place; Indianapolis, Indiana; City of Indiana (owner), Mansur Real Estate Services, Inc., and King Park Area Development Corporation (developers) ▪ First Ward Place/The Garden District; Charlotte, North Carolina; City of Charlotte (owner), Banc of America Community Development Corporation (master developer) ▪ The Fullerton Square Project; Singapore; Far East Organization/Sino Land ▪ Playhouse Square Center; Cleveland, Ohio; Playhouse Square Foundation ▪ The Plaza at PPL Center; Allentown, Pennsylvania; Liberty Property Trust ▪ Technology Square at Georgia Institute of Technology; Atlanta, Georgia; Georgia Institute of Technology and Georgia Tech Foundation (owners), Jones Lang LaSalle (development

manager) ▪ University Park at MIT; Cambridge, Massachusetts; Forest City Enterprises, City of Cambridge Community Development Department, and Massachusetts Institute of Technology ▪ Walt Disney Concert Hall; Los Angeles, California; Los Angeles County (owner), Walt Disney Concert Hall, Inc. (developer) ▪ WaterColor; Seagrove Beach, Florida; The St. Joe Company

2004 Europe: *Introduction of separate European awards program* ▪ Brindleyplace; Birmingham, United Kingdom; Argent Group, PLC ▪ Bullring; Birmingham, United Kingdom; The Birmingham Alliance ▪ Casa de les Punxes; Barcelona, Spain; Inmobiliaria Colonial ▪ Diagonal Mar; Barcelona, Spain; Hines Interests España ▪ Promenaden Hauptbahnhof Leipzig; Leipzig, Germany; ECE Projektmanagement GmbH & Co., Deutsche Bahn AG, and DB Immobilienfonds ▪ Regenboogpark; Tilburg, The Netherlands; AM Wonen

2005 The Americas: 34th Street Streetscape Program; New York, New York; 34th Street Partnership ▪ 731 Lexington Avenue/One Beacon Court; New York, New York; Vornado Realty Trust ▪ Heritage Award: The Chautauqua Institution; Chautauqua, New York; The Chautauqua Institution ▪ Fourth Street Live!; Louisville, Kentucky; The Cordish Company ▪ The Glen; Glenview, Illinois; The Village of Glenview and Mesirow Stein Real Estate, Inc. ▪ Harbor Town; Memphis, Tennessee; Henry Turley Company and Belz Enterprises ▪ The Market Common, Clarendon; Arlington, Virginia; McCaffery Interests, Inc. ▪ **Millennium Park;** Chicago, Illinois; City of Chicago and Millennium Park, Inc. ▪ Pueblo del Sol; Los Angeles, California; The Related Companies of California, McCormack Baron Salazar, The Lee Group, and Housing Authority of the City of Los Angeles ▪ Time Warner Center; New York, New York; The Related Companies, LP ▪ Ville Plácido Domingo; Acapulco, Mexico; Casas Geo and CIDECO-Anáhuac

2005 Europe: Cézanne Saint-Honoré; Paris, France; Société Foncière Lyonnaise and Predica ▪ Danube House; Prague, Czech Republic; Europolis Real Estate Asset ▪ Government Offices Great George Street; London, United Kingdom; Stanhope, PLC, and Bovis Lend Lease ▪ De Hoftoren; The Hague, The Netherlands; ING Real Estate Development ▪ Meander; Amsterdam, The Netherlands; Het Oosten Kristal and Latei

2005 Asia Pacific: *Introduction of separate Asia Pacific awards program* ▪ Federation Square; Melbourne, Australia; Federation Square Management ▪ **Hangzhou Waterfront;** Hangzhou, China; Hangzhou Hubin Commerce & Tourism Company, Ltd. ▪ The Loft; Singapore; CapitaLand Residential, Ltd. ▪ **Marunouchi Building;** Tokyo, Japan; Mitsubishi Estate Company, Ltd. ▪ Pier 6/7, Walsh Bay; Sydney, Australia; Mirvac Group and Transfield Holdings Pty, Ltd.

2005 ULI Global Awards for Excellence Winners

CONTENTS

COMMERCIAL

AGBAR TOWER

Barcelona, Spain

Development Team

Developer

**Layetana Developments
Barcelona, Spain
www.layetana.com**

Owner

**Agbar Group
Barcelona, Spain
www.agbar.es**

Architect

**Atelier Jean Nouvel
Paris, France
www.jeannouvel.fr**

Associate Architect

**b720 Arquitectos
Barcelona, Spain
www.b720.com**

Structural Engineer

**Brufau, Obiol, Moya & Associates, S.L.
Barcelona, Spain
www.bomasl.com**

The new 35-story headquarters of the Agbar Group, a Spanish multinational holding company, stands out like a lighthouse against the Barcelona skyline. Agbar Tower (Torre Agbar) is the cornerstone for new development in the new "22@ district," an emerging neighborhood that is transforming 198 hectares (489 ac) of Barcelona's 19th-century industrial Poblenou district into a 21st-century mixed-use district for the global knowledge-based industry. Its location alone, at the 22@ district's apex closest to Plaça de les Glòries Catalanes—the remarkable double-decker roundabout at the intersection of three of Barcelona's major boulevards (Gran Via, Diagonal, and Meridiana avenues)—accords Agbar Tower a landmark status. The multicolored, bullet-shaped tower contains 50,903 square meters (547,915 sf) of space, including 33,210 square meters (357,469 sf) of office space in 32 above-ground stories and 17,693 square meters (190,446 sf) of parking, an auditorium, a service area, and a loading bay on three subterranean levels. The total investment cost was €120 million.

The tower's shape is multireferential, leaving it open to many different interpretations. Its designer, French architect Jean Nouvel, calls it "a fluid mass that has perforated the ground," a permanent geyser reflecting the primary business activity of its owner, which provides water to the city of Barcelona and other municipalities in Spain and elsewhere. The structure's shape also mirrors that of Montserrat, a mountain that is a powerful symbol for the Catalan people. Finally, the tower pays homage to one of Catalonia's best-known architects, Antonio Gaudí. It is not, says Nouvel, a skyscraper; rather, "it is a unique growth" in the city: organic, like the architecture of Gaudí. And like Gaudí's architecture, Agbar Tower—despite its abstracted appearance and organic inspiration—also honors Western architectural traditions. Like a classical column, it rises perpendicularly from its plinth until, halfway up, it starts a gradual inward curve, following the entasis of a classical column. In that respect, it dispels comparison with Norman Foster's contemporaneous Swiss Re Tower in London, which is some six stories taller (Agbar Tower is currently Barcelona's third tallest building).

Agbar Tower consists of two nonconcentric ovoid cylinders, a larger one built around a smaller one, crowned with a steel and glass dome. The entire facade is made up of 92.5-square-centimeter (14.3 in²) modules; each story's perimeter is 120 modules around and four modules high. The three-layer facade features, from inside out, a first layer of concrete; a second of corrugated aluminum sheets of different colors—ranging from warmer tones at the bottom, representing the earth, to cooler tones above, representing the sky—and a third layer of more than 59,600 reflective, tinted glass louvers that blur the tones of the skin below, modifying its colors according to the time of day and the weather. (More than 4,500 separate lights on the building's exterior illuminate it at night, providing even more different colors and

Project Data

Web Page

www.layetana.com/english/procorp_
torreagbar.htm

Site Area

4,567 square meters (1.13 ac)
76 percent open space

Facilities

33,210 square meters (sf) gross
building area
330 subterranean parking spaces

Land Uses

office, parking

Start/Completion Dates

January 2001–June 2005

Jury Statement

Located at the intersection of three of Barcelona's most important streets, Agbar Tower stands out as a "lighthouse" for the city's burgeoning 22@ district. Containing 35 stories of office space and named for the company that occupies it, the tower incorporates a number of low-tech passive cooling techniques that belie its striking high-tech appearance.

patterns.) The building's open-plan interior, with no internal pillars, allows for an extremely efficient use of space, and its interior spaces are as colorful as its facade.

Layetana Developments' goal, from the start of the design process, was to keep the tower deliberately low-tech and energy-efficient. A walkway on the exterior of each story enables relatively unskilled workers to clean the structure from the outside every three months, and the triple epidermis improves its energy efficiency. While the building's 4,400 windows appear to be randomly distributed, they are more abundant on the northern face than the southern one, ensuring adequate ventilation and allowing the building's users to make optimal use of natural lighting.

The construction process, which began in January 2001, faced numerous challenges. Because the existing water table began just eight meters (26 ft) below street level, 30 wells had to be dug, and it took almost a year of round-the-clock pumping to drain the site sufficiently to construct the 45-meter-deep (158 ft) foundation. The 144.4-meter-high (473.7 ft) tower was built in three phases, using a self-climbing framework system. First came the inner ring, then the outer ring, and finally the elevator shafts. Mounting the dome also was a complex process. The general public, as well as local and international media, closely followed the building's progress; even before its completion, the tower was the most talked-about new building in the city.

Since the Agbar Group's 1,200 employees moved into the tower in June 2005, more than 50 other large, multinational firms have set up business in the surrounding district. (Numerous skyscrapers are being planned in the vicinity to meet demand in a city that is squeezed between the mountains and the sea.) "It has been one of the main driving forces in the new 22@ district explosion; it has become a new icon for the city of Barcelona, and today it is also a brand" for Agbar, says Jordi Mateu, Layetana's marketing and development manager.

BERGOGNONE 53

Milan, Italy

Named after its address in Milan's Porta Genova neighborhood, Bergognone 53 is a refurbishment of four nondescript buildings, in effect turning them into an important landmark in the rejuvenating neighborhood. A marquee tenant was secured, setting off an influx of fashion, media, and advertising studios that has branded Porta Genova as a fashionable neighborhood. Environmentally friendly mechanical systems were installed, which reinforced the project's with-it image while qualifying it for tax breaks.

Porta Genova is a well-located neighborhood—close to downtown and to the nightlife found in the Navigli canal district and served well by transportation, including the ring road around Milan and other highways, subways, and its own train station (Porta Genova, two blocks away). In 2000, however, it was characterized by obsolete industrial buildings, many of them abandoned. Hines bought four of these buildings at the southeast corner of the piazza at the intersection of Bergognone and Tortona streets—from the Italian postal service, which once had had its regional headquarters there—in a six-way bidding process that started at €110 million ($103 million). These were not historic buildings, and it would have been easier and cheaper to tear them down rather than to renovate them. But building regulations prohibited the addition of new floor space, and there were no design precedents in Porta Genova for new construction. Hines decided that refurbishment would be more in keeping with the character of the neighborhood.

Hines conducted an international architectural competition among 11 firms, won by Mario Cucinella Architects (MCA Integrated Design). MCA's design called for a glass canopy to cover the 900 square meters (9,688 sf) of open space between the four 1960s buildings, thus linking them visually and functionally. The steel and glass in the canopy and the bright colors of the exterior walls relate to the original industrial design of these and nearby buildings. Photovoltaic cells on the roof of one of the buildings add another industrial reference and generate electricity for common area lighting, earning Hines a grant of €87,000 ($107,000) from the regional Lombardian government.

Having pursued international credit tenants from the start, Hines signed Deloitte to a 12-year lease while the project was still under construction. To serve Deloitte's workforce of 1,600 employees at Bergognone 53 as well as other people in Porta Genova, the developer incorporated a number of amenities, including a daycare center, two restaurants, and underground parking for 100 cars. The four-building complex could be easily partitioned for four or more tenants, though Deloitte remains the sole tenant.

Since the project's completion in 2004, a number of industrial buildings in Porta Genova have been converted to mixed use. With Giorgio Armani moving its headquarters studio (designed by Tadao Ando) next door to Bergognone 53, Porta Genova—thanks in large part to the highly visible Bergognone 53—is gathering momentum as Milan's new hip neighborhood.

Development Team

Owner/Developer

Hines Italia, Srl.
Milan, Italy
www.hines.com

Architect

MCA Integrated Design, Srl.
Bologna, Italy
www.mcarchitects.it

Project Data

Web Site

www.bergognone53.com

Site Area

0.5 hectare (1.26 ac)
18 percent open space

Facilities

22,000 square meters (236,800 sf)
total building area

14,500 square meters (156,082 sf)
leasable office space

2,000 square meters (21,529 sf)
leasable retail space

80 subterranean parking spaces

Land Uses

office, retail/restaurant, open space (courtyards), parking

Start/Completion Dates

March 2002–December 2004

HYATT CENTER

Chicago, Illinois

Development Team

Owners/Developers

Higgins Development Partners
Chicago, Illinois
www.higginsdevelopment.com

Pritzker Realty Group
Chicago, Illinois

Design Architect

Pei Cobb Freed & Partners
Architects, LLP
New York, New York
www.pcf-p.com

Architect of Record

A. Epstein & Sons, International
Chicago, Illinois
www.epstein-isi.com

Landscape Architect

Peter Lindsay Schaudt Landscape
Architecture, Inc.
Chicago, Illinois
www.schaudt.ws

The first high-rise office tower to be built in downtown Chicago in the post-9/11 era, Hyatt Center incorporates state-of-the-art security and armoring systems while remaining open and accessible. Located at the northeast corner of South Wacker Drive and West Monroe Street, the 49-story, 1,765,000-square-foot (163,969 m²) structure is an unusual combination of build-to-suit and speculative office space. It also is the first Chicago building for the internationally known design firm Pei Cobb Freed & Partners.

Hyatt Center is the result of a strategic approach focused on creating build-to-suit environments for three high-profile corporate tenants as well as speculative space. Each of the lead tenants demanded innovative building solutions: Hyatt Corporation (300,000 sf/27,871 m²) wanted a seven-story internal atrium, Goldman Sachs (270,000 sf/25,084 m²) required substantial security enhancements and long-span trading floors, and the law firm Mayer, Brown, Rowe and Maw (475,000 sf/44,129 m²) asked for deep natural light penetration. A synergistic design and development process—involving the development team of Higgins Development Partners and Pritzker Realty Group; the three lead tenants; Pei Cobb Freed; and architect of record and engineer A. Epstein & Sons—ensured that all parties' needs were met.

A lozenge-shaped floor plan stretching the full length of the site—which is relatively narrow and hemmed in on two sides by neighboring office towers—maximizes floor area while optimizing views from the structure. Hyatt Center's elegant form, with its gently curving stainless steel and glass facade, sets it apart from—while fitting into—Chicago's rectilinear grid street pattern, serving tenants and the public alike by expanding views and access to natural light, both within the building and at street level. The curved form also creates pocket parks at either end of the building, providing oases of green space for the thousands of commuters who walk by the building daily. To complement these parks, recessed glass walls offer views into the extensively landscaped ground-floor lobby, making the public realm appear even larger and more inviting.

Hyatt Center's curved form increases efficiency. An interior bamboo forest, green roof, highly efficient glass, and state-of-the-art mechanical systems demonstrate the developer's commitment to sustainable design, and the building was the first commercial high rise to meet the city's new energy code. The building contractor undertook extensive recycling during the demolition and construction processes, and used a unitized curtain wall system to speed the enclosure process and minimize the need for supplementary heating during construction. Innovative design solutions also help ensure the safety of tenants and visitors: the exterior parks buffer the structure from vehicles, screening lobbies are located outside the structural frame, a concrete core offers emergency egress, package and mail screening facilities are isolated from public areas, and the building skin is blast resistant.

COMMERCIAL · FINALIST

Project Data

Web Page

www.hyattcenterinfo.com

Site Area

1.6 acres (6,475 m²)
22 percent open space

Facilities

49 floors above ground

1,765,000 square feet (163,969 m²)
gross building area

1,470,000 square feet (136,563 m²)
gross leasable area

250 subterranean parking spaces

Land Uses

office, parking

Start/Completion Dates

December 2002–January 2005

"A large high-rise office building needs to do more than contribute to the skyline," comments Jack Higgins, chairman and CEO of Higgins Development Partners. "It also has a responsibility to be a good citizen at the building's base. We believe that Harry Cobb's design accomplishes both with its unique oval shape and the ground-level open park structure." Although meeting the needs of three Class A tenants while also retaining flexibility as a speculative office tower was one of the most significant obstacles to Hyatt Center's successful development, in the end this complexity became one of its greatest strengths. The project has transformed a deteriorating parking lot into a structure that will pay up to $15 million in taxes annually. The development successfully balances world-class design with the realities of a challenging economic and financial environment. It makes a significant contribution to the community while reinforcing business's continued commitment to downtown Chicago.

LOURESHOPPING

Lisbon, Portugal

Development Team

Owner/Developer

Sonae Sierra
Lisbon, Portugal
www.sonaesierra.com

Project Architect

José Quintela da Fonseca
Lisbon, Portugal

Design Architect

Development Design Group, Inc.
Baltimore, Maryland
www.ddg-usa.com

Associate Architect

Intergaup
Alges, Portugal
www.intergaup.pt

LoureShopping is an innovative "green" shopping and leisure center that demonstrates its commitment to environmentally responsible development by including a large public park and green space and by meeting International Organization for Standardization (ISO) 14001 standards. It is the first shopping center in Portugal to obtain ISO 14001 certification for its construction phase, and more than 60 percent of the 8.29-hectare (20.5 ac) site is public green space. The center's 38,640-square-meter (415,917 sf) gross leasable area contains 121 shops (including a hypermarket and seven other anchor stores), 26 restaurants, and a seven-screen, 1,370-seat cinema, plus 2,100 surface parking spaces. The five-hectare (12.5 ac) park, which is accessible to the public as well as shoppers, includes more than 1,000 trees and other low-water-use plants, plus a pedestrian trail with a fitness course and exercise equipment, a bike trail, a sports field, and an open area for other outdoor events. A stream that coursed across the site was retained and incorporated into the public park; five wood bridges cross it as part of the pedestrian and bicycle trail systems.

Based on its experience as a shopping center developer and operator, Sonae Sierra created a set of Environmental Standards of Retail Development (ESRD) to guide LoureShopping's design and construction. The ESRD details approximately 160 environmental requirements that aim to minimize a project's impact on the environment, both during construction and throughout the center's life. It promotes waste recycling, the reduction of water use, energy efficiency, indoor air quality, and pollution prevention. In addition to meeting ISO 14001 standards for environmentally sound development practices, LoureShopping also is the first shopping center in Portugal to meet the Asociación Española de Normalización y

Certificación UNE 170001-2:2001 standards for universal accessibility by limiting physical barriers to movement and providing high-quality lighting.

Started in September 2003 and completed in October 2005, LoureShopping represents a €67 million investment that has created 1,000 new jobs. Two months after it opened, it was independently valued at €109 million, representing a 71 percent margin on investment. The center serves a market area of more than 640,000 people living within a 30-minute radius and meets their shopping, entertainment, and leisure needs by offering a diverse range of stores as well as restaurants, cinemas, and green space.

Designed by José Quintela, Sonae Sierra's senior manager for conceptual development and architecture, and the Baltimore, Maryland–based Development Design Group, Inc., the center, with its elegantly sweeping lines and smooth curves, presents a colorful blue, gold, and white exterior featuring sun and moon symbols that are repeated throughout the interior in hanging icons and sculptures, on walls, and in floor tiles and mosaics. Much of LoureShopping is lit by large windows and skylights, giving it a bright, airy ambience. It also features cutting-edge technology, including automated fire and intrusion detection systems as well as closed-circuit cable television monitoring. As Fernando Oliveira, executive director of European developments for Sonae Sierra, notes, "LoureShopping is a next-generation shopping and leisure center that represents a step forward in terms of innovation and quality, as well as in its shopping and leisure offerings. It abides by all of Sonae Sierra's rigorous demands in terms of comfort, safety, integration into the surrounding environment, and environmental quality."

Project Data

Web Page
www.loureshopping.pt

Site Area
8.29 hectares (20.5 ac)
60 percent open green space

Facilities
119,552 square meters (1,286,847 sf) gross building area

38,640 square meters (415,917 sf) gross leasable area

2,100 surface parking spaces

Land Uses
retail, public open space, parking

Start/Completion Dates
September 2003–October 2005

TREASURE ISLAND
PARK

MONTAGE RESORT AND SPA

Laguna Beach, California

For more than 50 years, a bluff-top site offering some of California's most spectacular ocean views was a gated trailer park for 268 mobile homes. The 30-acre (12 ha) site was not only an eyesore filled with increasingly dilapidated structures; it also prevented much-desired public access to the beach. Although as many as 37 developers tried to develop the land over the years, the community consistently opposed these plans, even after the mobile home park closed in 1996. Locals knew the oceanfront site as "Treasure Island," after the movie that was filmed there in 1934.

Enter the Athens Group, a developer experienced in creating complex, environmentally sensitive resort projects. It purchased the site in 1998 and worked closely with the city to develop a plan that ultimately included a 262-room luxury hotel and spa, 14 residential villas, 14 estate lots, and 14 acres (6 ha) of common open space, including a 7.25-acre (2.9 ha) public park. After a five-year entitlement process involving more than 42 public hearings, two referendums, and two rounds of California Coastal Commission approvals, the developer obtained all necessary approvals. This included rare unanimous approval from the Coastal Commission, which called the plan a "model for developers."

Before beginning the design process, the developer evaluated the land's distinctive features, as well as the area's culture and history, with the aim of creating a compatible property that would evoke a strong sense of place. The resulting Montage Resort and Spa, which opened in February 2003, is an environmentally and culturally sensitive resort that makes the most of its highly desirable coastal views and prime location while providing beach access for the entire community. Designed to honor Laguna Beach's artistic heritage, the resort's architecture embraces California Arts and Crafts design with a casual twist that incorporates a lighter color palette in addition to dark wood and stone. An 80-page design guidelines manual for estate lot buyers ensures that the custom homes are compatible with the hotel and villas. An arts program integrates nearly $1 million in public art throughout the property.

In its previous incarnation as a trailer park, without a hookup to the city sewer system, untreated waste went directly into the ocean. Now Montage treats its own site-generated sewage, as well as urban runoff from 60 additional acres of urban development uphill from the resort. The hotel commands one of the highest room rates (with an average daily rate of more than $500 a night) and occupancy levels of any luxury coastal property in southern California, significantly outperforming its competitors, and yields more than $4 million annually in visitor taxes for the city. It has been a clear financial success for the

Development Team

Owner/Developer

The Athens Group
Laguna Beach, California
www.athensdevco.com

Site Planner and Architect (Residential)

McLarand Vasquez Emsiek & Partners
Irvine, California
www.mve-architects.com

Architect (Hotel)

Hill Glazier Architects
Palo Alto, California
www.hillglazier.com

Project Data

Web Page

www.montagelagunabeach.com

Site Area

30 acres (12 ha)

47 percent public/common open space

Facilities

490,000 square feet (45,521 m²)
gross building area

28 residential units (14 completed)

262 hotel rooms

70 public/409 private parking spaces

Land Uses

hotel, residential, public park, parking

Start/Completion Dates

Purchased 1998–2003

Jury Statement

Montage Resort and Spa is an outstanding model for rehabilitating an underused property and returning it to productive use, benefiting the owner, the resort's guests, and the public. The developer converted a 30-acre (12 ha), gated trailer park, with no public access to ocean views or to the beach, into a five-star resort hotel and villas, opening its grounds and restored beach to the community. In addition, the developer demonstrated respect for the local arts and crafts heritage and created a public park as well as parking.

owner/developer, producing more than $115 million in residential sales and leaving the investors with a zero basis in land cost.

The centerpiece of the Montage's land use plan is the public park, which the developer designed in conjunction with the city and with community and environmental groups. The Athens Group built the park and an associated public parking structure for a cost of $9 million with no cash outlay from the city; the developer advanced these costs, which are being repaid through hotel occupancy taxes. The hotel operator, Montage Hotels & Resorts, pays all park maintenance costs. In addition to creating the park, the developer implemented a state-of-the-art water treatment system, restored a sandy beach, removed an old concrete platform on the beach, and built a rock jetty to protect the beach from erosion, creating a new tidal habitat that is now a state marine park.

"Ultimately, for us to be successful," notes Kim Richards, chief executive officer and president of the Athens Group, "it was essential that the local community embrace the resort as its own. And, in fact, the community is proud of the resort. Members of the community use it; they bring their families and friends there. It has evolved into an economic and social focal point in the community as well as a successful and vibrant resort."

POTSDAMER PLATZ ARKADEN

Berlin, Germany

Development Team

Owner/Developer

**DaimlerChrysler Immobilien GmbH
Berlin, Germany
www.daimlerchrysler-immobilien.de**

Project Manager

**ECE Projektmanagement GmbH
and Company KG
Hamburg, Germany
www.ece.de**

Architect

**ECE Architects
Hamburg, Germany
www.ece.de/en/index.jsp**

Master Planner

**Renzo Piano Building Workshop
Genoa, Italy
www.rpbw.com**

Potsdamer Platz, in the heart of Berlin, symbolizes the nation's reunification and points the way into the future for this old and new capital. Before it was reduced to rubble during World War II—and later cut in half by the construction of the Berlin Wall—the square was a shining symbol for the metropolis. After the war, the square remained a no-man's-land until the reunification of East and West Germany. The demolition of the wall presented a compelling opportunity to revive the square with a totally new mix of uses, and the area around the square became the largest building site in Europe. The new federal government assigned the largest of four quadrants to a development team led by what is now the Daimler-Chrysler Group. Between 1993 and 1998, a completely new urban district arose around Potsdamer Platz—office buildings, apartments, shops, and cultural institutions—characterized by striking modern architecture and civic planning concepts. At the southwest corner of this new district is Potsdamer Platz Arkaden, a three-level, 40,000-square-meter (430,556 sf) retail center.

Managed by ECE Projektmanagement GmbH and Company on behalf of debis Immobilienmanagement (DaimlerChrysler Group), with the cooperation of public authorities, the Potsdamer Platz Arkaden houses more than 120 shops, restaurants, and cafés. The developers' ambitious goal—to integrate this new shopping boulevard into the heart of the district, filling it with bustling life that would make it attractive to residents and visitors, large companies and independent businesses, and investors and retailers from within Berlin and beyond—clearly has been achieved.

Italian architect Renzo Piano's design guidelines produced a transparent complex of glass, brick, ceramics, and terra-cotta. A 16-meter-high (53 ft) glazed space-framed roof spans the 180-meter-long (591 ft) shopping boulevard, which follows the square's original street pattern and is open to the public 24 hours a day, seven days a week. This covered boulevard runs from north to south, ensuring access to natural daylight, which is softened in the southern section by glass surfaces covered with graphic prints. A double row of trees set in planting beds within the Arkaden also reinforces the avenue atmosphere. Because of its central location, city officials were closely involved in the project's planning, particularly with regard to infrastructure and traffic access. A new tram station was built to allow direct access to the city's tram system from the basement of the Arkaden, and a direct link to a planned regional railway station will be added in the future. The center also contains parking for 4,000 cars on three basement levels and in a nearby multistory structure.

COMMERCIAL · WINNER

Project Data

Web Page

www.ece.de/en/shopping/center/pob/pob.jsp

Site Area

1.6 hectares (4 ac)

Facilities

40,000 square meters (430,556 sf) gross building area

4,000 surface parking spaces

Land Uses

retail, public transit, parking

Start Date

October 1998

Jury Statement

At the symbolic center of Berlin, Potsdamer Platz represents both cold war friction and the subsequent reunification of Germany. With its enclosed shopping boulevard—creating 40,000 square meters (430,556 sf) of retail space—and its connection to a new train station, the Arkaden revitalizes Potsdamer Platz as the city's crossroads of culture, society, commerce, and politics.

All the Potsdamer Platz Arkaden's shops are fully leased, and demand for retail space is high, in recognition of the center's above-average sales volumes. The Arkaden created approximately 1,000 new jobs in the center of Berlin, and more than 50,000 people have visited it on an average day since it opened in October 1998. Notes Alexander Otto, CEO of ECE Projektmanagement, "Potsdamer Platz Arkaden is the vibrant heart of the new Berlin central district. Thanks to a successful blend of international flair and local Berlin character, the complex is seen as an outstanding example of a flourishing urban entertainment center and of the creation of a new and lively city center district."

TOUR CBX

Paris la Défense, France

Located on what was one of the last remaining sites in the La Défense high-rise business district just west of Paris, Tour CBX (CBX Tower) projects an iconic image while providing a high-quality working environment and making efficient use of a site constrained by its small size and by view-corridor restrictions. The 44,000-square-meter (473,612 sf) tower's footprint occupies half of the site's 2,400 square meters (25,833 sf). An innovative podium and elliptical floor-plate design provide up to 1,500 square meters (16,146 sf) of space on each of the 34 upper floors.

La Défense, girdled by an inner ring road and by the Seine beyond the city limits of Paris, has been reinventing itself as a commercial district since the 1950s. In 1972, outraged by the construction of the 58-story Tour Montparnasse in Paris's historic 15th arrondissement, the national government banned future skyscrapers in the city center, directing new towers to outlying La Défense. The new business district was accorded greater status with the construction of a symbolic center, La Grande Arche, marking the western terminus of the historical axis of Paris that aligns the Louvre, the Arc de Triomphe, and the Champs-Élysées. Today 150,000 people work in Paris la Défense's 3.5 million square meters (37 million sf) of office space, making it the largest CBD in Europe and the continent's busiest transportation hub.

Developer Tishman Speyer worked closely with the local planning authority—the Public Establishment for the Installation of La Défense (EPAD)—and architects Kohn Pedersen Fox Associates to ensure that the project would have a positive impact on the surrounding area and the Parisian skyline. The designers aimed to create a landmark tower that would provide maximum flexibility for the speculative office building's prospective tenants as well as a prestigious corporate image. The result is an asymmetric, bladelike design that provides flexible floor plates as well as a striking, 14-meter-high (46 ft) entrance plaza, an elegant reception area, natural stone floors and walls, and extensive glazing. The four-story podium houses public and retail services, a 550-seat restaurant, and a 100-seat cafeteria; the podium facade is completely transparent, providing extensive natural light while increasing visibility and drawing passersby into the building.

At 142 meters (466 ft), Tour CBX is Paris la Défense's 14th tallest skyscraper. Its lowest office floor is on level five, which is at the same height as the tenth floor of adjacent buildings. The tower is chilled by ceiling-mounted fan-coil air-handling units. A security station provides closed-circuit television monitoring, and access to all private areas is controlled by electronic badges. The structure was the first in France to feature destination-control elevators linked to the access identification system. These elevators are so efficient that only two banks of five elevators were required, reducing the size of the core and increasing the size and improving the efficiency of the floor plates. Additional amenities include room

Development Team

Owner

Dexia Crédit Local
Paris la Défense, France
www.dexia-clf.fr

Developer

Tishman Speyer
Paris, France
www.tishmanspeyer.com

Design Architect

Kohn Pedersen Fox Associates, PC
New York, New York
www.kpf.com

Associate Architect

SRA Architectes
Châtillon, France
www.sra-architectes.com

Project Data

Web Page
www.tishmanspeyer.com/properties/
Property.aspx?id=8

Site Area
2,400 square meters (25,833 sf)

Facilities
44,000 square meters (473,612 sf) gross
building area

38,500 square meters (414,424 sf) net
leasable office area

13 structured parking spaces

Land Uses
office, parking

Start/Completion Dates
January 2003–September 2005

Jury Statement

Built as a speculative office tower on
one of the last remaining sites in the
high-rise La Défense business district
of Paris, Tour CBX was sold to its
primary tenant. The development team
overcame the problems of a difficult
site to produce an elegant 34-story
tower that projects an iconic image
and provides an exceptional working
environment.

service and connections to La Défense's fiber-optic communications system. A double-height top floor offers impressive executive office space and exceptional views of Paris.

Construction began in January 2003 and was completed in September 2005 at a total development cost of €280 million, including the cost of the land. Shortly thereafter, in December 2005, the French-Belgian banking group Dexia Crédit Local purchased the building to serve as its regional headquarters.

VICTORIA GARDENS

Rancho Cucamonga, California

Located in southern California's fast-growing Inland Empire, Victoria Gardens provides a new downtown for an evolving community. With a mix of upscale retail offerings, cultural and civic facilities, professional offices, and housing built on a traditional street grid system featuring a large town square, informal pocket parks, courtyards, sidewalks, and pedestrian paseos, Victoria Gardens has created a sense of place in a locale previously known mainly as a spillover area for urban growth from Los Angeles and Orange counties. On a 175-acre (71 ha) site, more than 1.8 million square feet (167,220 m²) of retail space, 45,000 square feet (4,181 m²) of office space, more than 500 residential units, and 6,900 parking spaces will make Victoria Gardens, when built out, one of the largest stand-alone main street projects in the United States when its final phase opens in 2008. (Phase I opened in 2004, and a second phase will be complete in September 2006.) The center also contains a 540-seat theater, a children's library, and a police substation.

Innovative approaches were needed to overcome four critical development challenges: pioneering lifestyle retailing in a changing region; underwriting large and atypical infrastructure improvements; solving design problems associated with an open-air plan meant to function as a town center for the city of Rancho Cucamonga; and negotiating a complex public/private transaction in a regulatory environment that ruled out many of the forms of public assistance typically used to develop such projects.

Forest City Commercial Development, a division of Forest City Enterprises, Inc., recognized that the improving demographics in the Inland Empire made it ripe for an upscale lifestyle center. But persuading retailers was not easy. In order to differentiate the project from nearby regional malls, Forest City settled on a mixed-use town center design that incorporates civic and cultural facilities as well as offices and housing. To create a sense of place, the project's back story explains how the community grew over time from a simple group of buildings along a farm road to a diverse main street locale. Four architectural firms were engaged to design buildings representing various historical periods. Some buildings were designed to look as if they had been converted from other uses to serve today's needs; others appear to be several small shops stacked next to each other. The result is a tapestry of structures, streetscapes, and landscaping that reflects the history of Rancho Cucamonga.

The development of Victoria Gardens would not have been possible without two critical public/private transactions. The first was for infrastructure financing. The cost of the necessary infrastructure improvements (which included almost $50 million worth of regional drainage and street improvements) had precluded the site's development for decades, and California law prevented the Rancho Cucamonga Redevelopment Agency from offering any form of assistance other than a land writedown. The creation

Development Team

Owner/Developer

Forest City Commercial Development
Los Angeles, California
www.forestcity.net

Limited Partner

Lewis Group of Companies
Upland, California
www.lewisop.com

Architects

Altoon + Porter
Los Angeles, California
www.altoonporter.com

Elkus/Manfredi Architects, Ltd.
Boston, Massachusetts
www.elkus-manfredi.com

Field Paoli Architects
San Francisco, California
www.fieldpaoli.com

KA Architecture
Cleveland, Ohio
www.architectureoflife.com

Designer

Redmond Schwartz Mark Design
San Clemente, California
www.rsmdesign.net

Landscape Architect

SWA Group
Laguna Beach, California
www.swagroup.com

Civil Engineer

MDS Consulting
La Quinta, California
www.mdsconsulting.net

of a community facilities district and the cooperation of the city and nearby landowners provided the financing that made these major infrastructure improvements possible. The second, more complex transaction involved the city's conveyance of the land to Forest City for $1. In return, the city, through its redevelopment agency, will participate in the project's future profits. The total development cost will be approximately $234 million.

In its first full year of operation, Victoria Gardens generated nearly $600 per square foot ($6,459 per m²) in retail sales and has spurred the development of more than 500,000 square feet (46,450 m²) of new retail space nearby. In addition to its prospective share of the profits, the city will benefit from the more than $5 million generated by the project annually in sales and property taxes. Victoria Gardens offers a model for how public agencies and private developers can work together to leap the hurdles that often stand in the way of a development of this scope and scale. It has become the heart of its community, as well as a regional shopping destination.

Project Data

Web Page

www.victoriagardensie.com

Site Area

175 acres (71 ha)

10 percent common open space

Facilities

1,200,000 square feet (111,480 m²)
gross leasable space

49,000 square feet (4,552 m²)
office area

300,000 square feet (27,870 m²)
retail area

90,000 square feet (8,361 m²)
civic spaces

56,000 square feet (5,202 m²) cinema

600 residential units

6,900 on-street parking spaces

1,180 structured parking spaces

Land Uses

retail, office, residential, entertainment, civic

Start/Completion Dates

August 2003–October 2004 (Phase I)

In the fast-growing Inland Empire region of southern California, Victoria Gardens provides a new town center for a suburban community that had grown up without one. The 175-acre (71 ha) project's back story reflects the region's agricultural heritage, and a successful mix and placement of retailers were made possible by the contemporary open-air configuration. The city's assistance in the form of nominal land costs and generous land writedowns in the absence of infrastructure subsidies has helped produce positive financial results for a creative public/private sharing arrangement.

MIXED USE

15–25 DAVIES STREET

London, United Kingdom

It is not often that a new project gets built in Mayfair, one of central London's most desirable residential neighborhoods. Much of the land here is owned by the Grosvenor Estate and is occupied under leaseholds that do not encourage the kind of teardown projects that rejuvenate other cities. And even when a property becomes available, the local Westminster planning authority has complete domain over what can be built. The planning authority would be expected to be particularly anxious about any development along Davies Street, which forms a southern gateway to Mayfair from Berkeley Square.

Given this restrictive environment, the design of 15–25 Davies Street is a surprise. But perhaps not that surprising because, despite its obvious parentage in modern architecture, the building blends in sensitively with its historic setting. In form, 15–25 Davies Street fits the archetype of a turn-of-the-century British mansion block, but it houses an up-to-date mix of uses that includes a restaurant at street level topped by two office floors and five residential stories. The building's materials are traditional as well, but they are used in decidedly modern ways.

The site is on a busy thoroughfare on the eastern fringe of Mayfair Village. Residents considered the previous 1960s structure that had occupied the site to be a misfit in the neighborhood. When the landowner offered the developer, Capital and City, a 50 percent interest in a joint venture and a 150-year leasehold for the redevelopment of the site, it was expected that the planning authority would insist on a historical—Victorian or Edwardian—building design. But the careful consideration that the developer gave to the architectural details of a proposed contemporary design—including the use of terra-cotta inside and out, filigreed glass-and-steel bays on the exterior, and steel stair balustrades on the interior—swayed the authority.

Separate entrances to the offices (15 Davies), residences (21 Davies), and restaurants (25 Davies) are on Davies Street, but are distinct from one another. Two levels of office space are directly above the street-level retail/restaurant space. The residential component comprises one two-bedroom unit sharing the second-story office level, four two- or three-bedroom flats on each of the three stories above the office stories, and two duplexes on the penthouse level. They feature multiple balconies, and the penthouse units have spacious garden terraces. The 16 parking spaces in the basement are reserved for residents. The residences have sold out, at a high average sale price of £14,693 per square meter ($2,500/£1,365 per sf). Venice's Cipriani restaurant preleased the ground-floor space for its London branch, and the office space was leased up within three months of the project's completion.

Development Team

Owner/Developer

Capital and City, PLC
London, United Kingdom

Architect

Kohn Pedersen Fox Associates
(International), PA
London, United Kingdom
www.kpf.co.uk

Project Data

Web Site

www.the21stmayfair.com

Site Area

743 square meters (8,000 sf)

Facilities

5,708 square meters (61,440 sf) total area

1,152 square meters (12,400 sf) leasable office space

650 square meters (7,000 sf) leasable restaurant space

14 for-sale residential units

16 parking spaces

Land Uses

restaurant, office, residential

Completion Date

August 2004

100 CAMBRIDGE STREET

Boston, Massachusetts

Development Team

Owner/Developer

**MassDevelopment/Saltonstall
Building Redevelopment Corporation
Boston, Massachusetts
www.massdevelopment.com**

Architect

**Elkus/Manfredi Architects, Ltd.
Boston, Massachusetts
www.elkus-manfredi.com**

Development Manager

**Meredith & Grew
Boston, Massachusetts
www.m-g.com**

Project Data

Web Pages

www.100cambridgestreet.com

www.bowdoinplace.com

Site Area

three acres (1.2 ha)

33 percent open space

The transformation of an abandoned government office building surrounded by bleak plazas into a vibrant, mixed-use complex of public and private offices, residences, retail shops, and gardens, 100 Cambridge Street has repaired the damage created by urban renewal in the 1960s, created critically needed housing, and provided new public green space. "The story of 100 Cambridge Street is one of public/private partnership at its best," says Robert L. Culver, president and CEO of MassDevelopment, the economic development agency for the commonwealth of Massachusetts. "The state legislature understood the importance and magnitude of this redevelopment project, and passed special legislation authorizing MassDevelopment to hire a top-notch development team. Today, 100 Cambridge is a model for smart growth redevelopment. In addition to revitalizing a prominent intersection at a gateway to a historic neighborhood, it is close to public transportation, draws thousands of workers and visitors daily, and is home to 75 families."

Built in 1965, the monolithic Leverett P. Saltonstall state office building replaced a neighborhood of 19th-century buildings at the foot of Boston's historic Beacon Hill. By the 1990s it had deteriorated badly, and asbestos used in the building's mechanical systems had become a health and liability hazard. Consequently, the state closed it in 1999. In November 1999, the Massachusetts Division of Capital Asset Management issued a request for proposals to renovate the structure. MassDevelopment teamed with three private companies to craft a response. Their proposal, which included a financial solution that would fund the redevelopment without affecting the commonwealth's general obligation bond cap, was accepted, and in 2000 the state legislature created the MassDevelopment/Saltonstall Building Redevelopment Corporation.

At the heart of the team's approach was the decision to preserve the existing tower rather than demolish it and start anew. The developer removed asbestos throughout the building and installed new energy-efficient windows, building systems, lobbies, and tenant finishes. Floors 13 through 22, which offer citywide views, have been programmed for private tenants, while the lower floors house state agencies. To complement the existing tower, add a mix of uses, and return activity to the streetscape, architects designed a five-story structure that wraps around the corners of the site. This plinth not only created streetfront retail space, upper-story residences, and a dramatic new office entrance, as well as residential townhouses and flats that complement the 19th-century residential buildings facing the site; it also added a

street presence that better relates 100 Cambridge Street to its urban neighborhood. The residences also enclose the tower's formerly barren, windswept plaza, which has been rebuilt as a public park and memorial garden. This design solution created 75 new homes (12 townhouses and 63 flats, 19 of which are affordable to low- and moderate-income households) in one of the nation's most expensive housing markets.

An innovative financing and legal structure ensures long-term benefits for the building's owner. The project is structured to provide the commonwealth with a below-market, fixed-price, long-term lease for 286,000 square feet (26,570 m²) of office space. Through an unusual ground lease arrangement (50 years, with two 15-year options), the private office space and retail space generate income for the commonwealth and eventually will be returned to it free of charge. By creating a master condominium with one public unit, one private commercial unit, and one residential unit, MassDevelopment was able to take advantage of tax-exempt bond financing for the public office space renovations while financing the private improvements through taxable bonds, at no cost to the commonwealth.

Today, despite the original tower's reputation as an unpleasant, depressing place—and a soft downtown office market—the office space is 97 percent leased at competitive market rents. All the residential condominiums have been sold—at an average price of $636 per square foot ($6,846/m²) for the market-rate units—and the retail space is occupied by a pharmacy, daycare center, and restaurant, returning 24-hour activity to the street. Once completely off the tax rolls, the property now generates more than $2 million in annual property taxes for the city of Boston.

Facilities

565,157 square feet (52,505 m²) leasable office space

34,539 square feet (3,209 m²) leasable retail space

75 total residential units: 56 market rate, 19 affordable

415 structured parking spaces

Land Uses

office, retail, residential, open space, parking

Start/Completion Dates

Spring 2002–June 2004

BELMAR

Lakewood, Colorado

Belmar, a 22-block downtown in the making, exemplifies the potential for transforming post–World War II bedroom suburbs into more diverse, compact, sustainable, pedestrian-oriented, and transit-oriented communities. When completed, it promises to be a model for the redefinition of suburban communities that have been buffeted by inexorable growth over the past several decades.

Lakewood, ten minutes west of Denver, is such a community. With a population approaching 150,000, it is Colorado's fourth largest city. In the early 1900s, wealthy Denver families built country estates there, the largest of which was Belmar. During and after World War II, growth spread west of Denver. In Lakewood, this was spurred by the opening of a federal munitions plant and the Denver Federal Center, which with 10,000 employees in 30 agencies is the largest federal compound outside the Washington, D.C., metropolitan area. In 1966, the 1.4 million-square-foot (130,000 m²) Villa Italia—the largest shopping mall in the mountain/plains region—opened to great fanfare and became, until its closing in 2001, Lakewood's de facto commercial and civic center.

Long before its actual demise, when it was 70 percent vacant, Villa Italia was clearly dying despite its high-traffic location (80,000 cars passing by its northwest corner each day). But efforts to redevelop it had foundered at the ballot box and been discouraged by a complicated ownership structure involving separate landowners, ground leases, and 140 lease subinterests. However, the process of trying to redevelop the mall had been a learning experience for city officials, who applied the lesson of public/private participation to form a 30-member Mayor's Villa Advisory Committee (to coordinate development activity) and establish the Lakewood Reinvestment Authority (to provide public financing and other urban renewal resources). Denver-based Continuum Partners was selected by the city as its development partner and worked with these public entities to obtain rezoning, permits, infrastructure financing, and condemnation of the underlying ground lease.

The redevelopment program aims to create for Lakewood a new, 22-block downtown—called Belmar, after the torn-down estate for which the area was famous. At buildout, which is projected for 2010 to 2012, the 104-acre (42 ha) site will contain 1.1 million square feet (102,193 m²) of retail, restaurant, and entertainment space; 800,000 square feet (74,322 m²) of office and hotel space; and 1,300 residential units in an urban mix of townhouses, lofts, live/work units, and condominium and rental apartments.

Phase I opened in May 2004. At the end of 2005, Belmar had 650,000 square feet (60,387 m²) of retail/restaurant/entertainment space, 84 percent leased, with rents that are comparable to regional mall rents, averaging $30 per square foot ($420 per m²), with common area management (CAM) charges in the range of $10 to $15 per square foot ($110 to $160 per m²). Belmar's 212,000 square feet (19,695 m²)

Development Team

Owner/Master Developer

Continuum Partners, LLC
Denver, Colorado
www.continuumpartners.com

Residential Developers

McStain Neighborhoods
Louisville, Colorado
www.mcstain.com

Trammell Crow Residential
Denver, Colorado
www.tcresidential.com

Public Partners

City of Lakewood
Lakewood, Colorado
www.lakewood.org

Lakewood Reinvestment Authority

Mayor's Villa Advisory Committee

Architects

Elkus Manfredi, Ltd.
Boston, Massachusetts
www.elkus-manfredi.com

Van Meter Williams Pollack
Denver, Colorado
www.vmwp.com

Architecture Denver
Denver, Colorado
www.architecturedenver.com

QPK Design
Syracuse, New York
www.qpkdesign.com

Shears Adkins Architects, LLC
Denver, Colorado
www.shearsadkins.com

Belzberg Architects
Santa Monica, California
www.belzbergarchitects.com

Landscape Architects

Civitas, Inc.
Denver, Colorado
www.civitasinc.com

EDAW, Inc.
Denver, Colorado
www.edaw.com

of office space is 90 percent occupied in a soft regional office market. Office space rents at or above the rates charged for the highest quality space in the suburban west-side Denver market.

Belmar's 109 rental units are 90 percent leased at $1.35 per square foot ($14 per m²), representing a $.20 to $.50 per square foot ($2.15 to $5.38 per m²) premium over comparable units in the submarket and almost equivalent to rents being achieved in some of central Denver's best locations. A joint venture with Trammell Crow Residential is adding 310 rental units and 75 loft-style condominiums. Phase I's condominium units sold at $245 to $310 per square foot ($2,637 to $3,337 per m²), and the first 70 rowhouses sold for an average price of more than $360,000. These Phase I results are unprecedented in the local market. Current sale prices for rowhouses average $380,000, and condominiums in a 62-unit building with ground-floor retail space are selling at $240,000 to $900,000.

This snapshot of leasing and sales activity demonstrates that interest is high and that people are beginning to take ownership of the Belmar concept. Currently under construction are 100,000 square feet (9,290 m²) of retail/restaurant/entertainment space and over 600 housing units.

All buildings in Belmar feature ground-level windows and doors on all sides to enhance the streetscape and the pedestrian experience. A segment of one street can be closed off temporarily to accommodate a public market. A 15,000-square-foot (1,394 m²) contemporary-arts center has been completed, as well as a two-acre (8,094 m²) urban park and three public parking structures. A multitenant, speculative office building has earned a silver certification from the U.S. Green Building Council's Leadership in Energy and Environmental Design (LEED) building rating program. Such features and design choices reflect Belmar's celebration of the public realm over the private realm. At Belmar, streets are more important than any buildings on them, and parks and plazas are more important than the buildings that surround them.

Project Data

Web Site

www.belmarcolorado.com

Site Area

104 acres (42 ha)

Facilities (at Buildout)

800,000 square feet (74,322 m²) leasable
office space and hotel

1.1 million square feet (102,193 m²)
leasable retail space

1,300 residential units

Land Uses

retail, entertainment, civic, office,
hotel, residential

Completion Dates

May 2004 for Phase I

2010–2012 buildout

Jury Statement

A public/private partnership envisioned
a dying 104-acre (42 ha) suburban mall
in Lakewood as the city's new downtown and now is transforming that
vision into reality by developing a much-
needed mixed-use, pedestrian-oriented
town center district. As it nears completion, Belmar is justifying the developer's tenacity in pioneering a new
urban lifestyle and neighborhood in a
place with no history or tradition of
embracing these alternatives.

CLAYTON LANE

Denver, Colorado

Development Team

Owner/Developer

The Nichols Partnership, Inc.
Denver, Colorado
www.nicholspartnership.com

Hotel Developers

Mortenson Development, Inc.
Minneapolis, Minnesota
www.mortenson.com

Sunstone Hotel Investors, Inc.
San Clemente, California
www.sunstonehotels.com

Architects

David Owen Tryba Architects, Inc.
Denver, Colorado
www.dota.com

RNL Design
Denver, Colorado
www.rnldesign.com

Shears Adkins Architects, LLC
Denver, Colorado
www.shearsadkins.com

Landscape Architect

Studio Insite, LLC
Denver, Colorado
www.studio-insite.com

Since the 1950s, the intersection of First Avenue and University Boulevard has been Denver's premier shopping location. Between December 2001 and March 2005, the Nichols Partnership, Inc., redeveloped 9.5 acres (3.85 ha) at the northeastern quadrant of the intersection, which had held freestanding Sears and Whole Foods stores and a surface parking lot, as Clayton Lane, a mixed-use project that combines 710,000 square feet (65,959 m²) of hotel, retail, office, and residential uses anchored by a new private street.

Clayton Lane is the last large parcel to be developed in land-constrained Cherry Creek. The project's unifying strength is 340,000 square feet (31,586 m²) of high-visibility retail space. A design palette featuring brick, limestone, zinc panels, chrome, and wood, combined with varied building facades and fenestration, creates distinctive storefronts. The development also contains a 170,000-square-foot (15,793 m²) corporate headquarters for Janus Capital Group; a four-star, 140,000-square-foot (13,006 m²), 196-room JW Marriott hotel; 25 luxury residential condominiums; and 1,648 parking spaces in two underground garages and an above-ground parking structure.

The development team faced a mountain of challenges, from initial neighborhood opposition to the difficulties of phasing and financing a $160 million, mixed-use project, to the demands of building on a particularly active, compact development site. The effort to have the property rezoned and to acquire entitlements and variances that allowed for the height and density necessary to support an office building and luxury hotel in Denver's most restrictive district required years of negotiations and extensive layers of approvals. Financing the project was a complex process, since it involved securing mixed-use construction financing from six different lenders in a turbulent real estate market and also required renegotiating existing leases and restructuring ownership into a complex planned community with dozens of units and multiple expense-sharing ratios and formulas. Finally, highly coordinated and proactive efforts were needed to keep the peace in the congested community during construction.

As an urban infill development, Clayton Lane is successful by all measures. Sales of office and residential components established new records for the city on a per-square-foot basis. The 2005 sale of the office tower eclipsed Denver's previous per-square-foot sales price by more than 50 percent. The residential condominiums sold quickly, at an average price of $435 per square foot ($4,683/m²). Retail leasing exceeded pro forma in a competitive market, and the retail space is fully leased. The JW Marriott Cherry Creek was Denver's most successful hotel in 2005, as measured by revenue per available room, room rates, and occupancy. In addition, Clayton Lane has been recognized by the U.S. Environmental Protection Agency for an innovative partnership with a local transportation management organization that enhances quality of life and economic vitality by reducing traffic congestion and improving mobility.

Project Data

Web Page

www.claytonlane.com

Site Area

9.5 acres (3.85 ha)

Facilities

223,000 square feet (20,717 m²)
gross office area

340,000 square feet (31,587 m²)
gross retail area

25 condominium units

196 hotel rooms

1,648 structured parking spaces

Land Uses

office, retail, residential, hotel,
parking

Start/Completion Dates

December 2001–March 2005

Clayton Lane has become a gateway to and the heart of Denver's most prominent upscale district, adding street life and new land uses to a previously underused site while resolving the neighborhood's parking and vehicular circulation shortcomings. "Clayton Lane presented a unique opportunity to combine high-quality retail, residential, office, and hotel uses on a dense urban infill site," notes Randy Nichols, president of the Nichols Partnership. "The beauty of Clayton Lane is that we were able to successfully integrate these uses into the distinctive fabric of Cherry Creek while raising the bar for high-quality infill development in Denver. The net result of this effort is a financially successful project that has become a key component of Cherry Creek's identity."

THE HERITAGE AT MILLENNIUM PARK

Chicago, Illinois

Development Team

Owners/Developers

Mesa Development, LLC
Chicago, Illinois

Walsh Investors, LLC
Chicago, Illinois

Klutznick-Fisher Development Company
Chicago, Illinois

Markwell Properties Development, Inc.
Hillside, Illinois

Architect

Solomon Cordwell Buenz
Chicago, Illinois
www.scb.com

Restoration Architect

McGuire Igleski & Associates
Evanston, Illinois
www.miarchitects.com

The Heritage at Millennium Park, a 57-story, two-tiered, 1.25 million-square-foot (116,125 m²) tower, has introduced luxury high-rise living to Chicago's Loop. Planning for the tower began in 2000, prior to the construction of Millennium Park and well before the park became an internationally renowned public space (and winner of a 2005 ULI Global Award for Excellence). The building makes a bold architectural statement on a site highly visible to the park's millions of visitors. Graceful curves and the intricately articulated exterior of the tower relate to the grand scale of the modern office buildings to the north, while its podium of four preserved and restored historic facades respect the 20th-century cornice lines of the pedestrian-level street wall to the south.

Seizing on the vision of city planners who announced the construction of Millennium Park, the development team, led by Mesa Development, LLC, assembled a complex site offering outstanding views—protected in perpetuity—of the future park. While the trend toward downtown living had not yet moved south of the Chicago River, the developers saw the opportunity to offer residents closer proximity to work and the city's cultural venues than any of the existing luxury neighborhoods north of the river. A sales center overlooking the park opened in July 2001, and 60 percent of the condominium units had been reserved by 9/11. Recognizing that the terrorist attacks had created concerns about high-rise living, the developer offered early buyers the opportunity to cancel their reservations, and 36 percent did. The developer continued the project and ultimately sold, in effect, 125 percent of the residences months before completion.

"Developing the Heritage at Millennium Park was a once-in-a-lifetime experience at a site that offered incredible opportunities—and presented a number of unusual obstacles, ranging from assembling nine separate parcels to overcoming a strong market perception that high-end homebuyers won't pay to live downtown," comments Richard Hanson, principal, Mesa Development. "Overall, this development required a giant leap of faith. We believed in the site, overlooking the unfinished Millennium Park, and believed in Mayor Daley's vision for a 24/7 downtown. We had one chance to make this property everything it could and should be for decades to come, and that's what we achieved. The enthusiastic response has led to a huge boom in downtown residential development that has been chronicled in everything from *Urban Land* magazine to the *New York Times.*"

Designed for flexibility, the Heritage features 358 residences with 27 different floor plans, ranging in size from 800 to 5,000 square feet (74 to 465 m²) and priced from approximately $300,000 to more than

$3 million, as well as 600 deeded parking spaces and 110,000 square feet (10,219 m²) of retail space. The approximate sellout value of the project is more than $300 million. Since their completion, the residences have appreciated significantly, producing a high return on investment for buyers as well as the developers. In addition, the project—which was developed without any public financing, tax credits, or incentives—will provide an estimated $6 million or more annually in incremental real estate taxes.

Environmental and historic restoration groups as well as architecture critics have hailed the Heritage for its excellent use of space and its preservation of the facades of four historic buildings. The project absorbed the $4 million cost of restoring the Wabash Street facades, which included reproducing intricate terra-cotta ornamentation from archival drawings and photographs, as well as cannibalizing face brick from a demolished building, and bracing the historic storefronts while construction went on behind them. Behind these storefronts are two levels of retail space and, above them, five levels of parking. Because the residential tower is set back from the street, pedestrians see only what appears to be five-story historic facades, looking much as they have since the area was redeveloped after the Great Chicago Fire of 1871.

Project Data

Web Page

www.heritagecondo.com

Site Area

40,000 square feet (3,716 m²)

Facilities

1,250,000 square feet (116,129 m²) gross building area

110,000 square feet (10,219 m²) retail area

358 condominium units

600 structured parking spaces

Land Uses

residential, retail, parking

Start/Completion Dates

December 2001–December 2004

IZUMI GARDEN

Tokyo, Japan

Izumi Garden is located in the Roppongi neighborhood of Minato ward, one of the five wards composing Tokyo's downtown core. The neighborhood, known for its nightlife and expatriate community, is characterized by a hilly topography. The 3.2-hectare (7.9 ac) site area above Roppongi i-chome ("i-chome" means first street) was owned by 60 proprietors and long-term leaseholders. These complications long prevented the site from being redeveloped for better land use.

The Sumitomo conglomerate's founding family, however, still owned its feudal estate here: a mansion that has been preserved as Sen-oku Hakuko Kan, part of the Izumi Garden complex, as a museum for the esteemed Sumitomo Collection of ancient Chinese artifacts. The museum faces the perfectly preserved 3,950-square-meter (42,517 sf) garden after which the Izumi Garden complex is named. (Izumi means "fountain," as in a natural hillside spring, from which water flows continuously in the ancestral garden.) From there, the site drops 20 meters (65.6 ft) to the Roppongi i-chome subway station.

In the late 1980s, the planning for the new subway station on Roppongi i-chome prompted Sumitomo Realty and Development Company, Ltd., to lead the assemblage of the site and propose a large-scale, mixed-use redevelopment within the guidelines of the recently approved District Renewal Program (DRP) for this area of Roppongi. As majority owner, Sumitomo led a joint venture including Mori Building Company, Ltd. (which developed the nearby Ark Hills, Atago Green Hills, and Roppongi Hills); because the project was being conducted under the auspices of the DRP, it bore the imprimatur of Tokyo's city planning program. This made it easier to coordinate the interests of the 60-plus owners and public and private stakeholders and to streamline the permitting process.

Izumi Garden was the first application of the DRP in Roppongi. Some of the benefits the program conveyed included a favorable floor/area ratio (FAR) allotment; an ability to negotiate with the transit company to coordinate the subway facility within the Izumi Garden project; and public subsidies for infrastructure costs. An FAR of 1,000 percent was allowed for the two towers closest to Roppongi i-chome, compared with an average of 120 percent prior to redevelopment. In negotiations with the subway company, Sumitomo was able to locate the new stop so that the concourse would open directly into the Izumi office tower. That seamlessness between building and subway station lobby enabled the building architect to design a configuration that lets natural light reach the subway lobby, three levels below grade, and permits movement of large numbers of people in and out of the building. Finally, the Minato ward government granted infrastructure subsidies that amounted to 6 percent of the total cost of development.

At the center of Izumi Garden, a cascading series of plazas rises from Roppongi i-chome to the museum and garden along what Sumitomo calls an "urban corridor." Terraced plazas, with shops tucked underneath

Development Team

Owner/Developer

Sumitomo Realty and Development Company, Ltd.
Tokyo, Japan
www.sumitomo-rd.co.jp

Codeveloper

Mori Building Company, Ltd.
Tokyo, Japan
www.mori.co.jp

Architect and
Landscape Architect

Nikken Sekkei
Tokyo, Japan
www.nikken.co.jp

Project Data

Web Page

www.sumitomo-rd.co.jp/izumi_garden

Site Area

3.2 hectares (7.9 ac)

34 percent open space

Facilities

208,002 square meters (2,238,915 sf) gross building area

83,300 square meters (896,633 sf) gross leasable office area

5,900 square meters (63,507 sf) retail area

261 residential units

189 hotel rooms

516 structured parking spaces

34 surface parking spaces

Land Uses

office, retail, residential, hotel, museum, open space, subway connection

Start/Completion Dates

October 1988–July 2002

Jury Statement

Over the years in a downtown Tokyo district, a large number of individually owned parcels with uneven topography had created an underused site. The developer painstakingly assembled the parcels and redeveloped them as a 3.2-hectare (7.9 ac), mixed-use project with a central spine of terraced plazas cascading down the hillside. Izumi Garden comprises office and residential towers, a hotel, a museum, a retail complex, a new subway concourse, and a preserved ancient private garden.

at each level, feature broad steps on one side and escalators on the other. On the south side of the urban corridor is the 45-story Izumi Garden Office Tower, the tallest building in Roppongi at the time construction was completed. On the corridor's north side is the 32-story, 260-unit Izumi Garden Residential Tower.

In one corner of the green-glazed office tower, a 16-meter by 16-meter (52.5 sq ft) flying atrium vertically connects 17 floors of offices to the subway lobby below ground. Two banks of glass-walled, high-speed elevators are visible within their superstructures. The office floors start at the seventh level, at the same level as the elevated expressway above Roppongi i-chome. Below the seventh-floor office lobby are the retail and restaurant levels, closer to the sidewalk and to the terraced urban corridor. A stacked, voided core, another unusual feature, permits easy access to mechanical and electrical equipment and permits a staging area for renovation and repairs.

The office tower was completed in July 2002 with undersubscribed lease commitments. In the following year, vacancy in Tokyo's five central wards increased, peaking at 6 to 8 percent. Sumitomo held out for its premium rents and tenants and was rewarded with an increase in demand in 2004. Izumi Garden is now fully leased. Moreover, its 189-room hotel reached an occupancy rate of 85 percent within its first six months of operations and has stabilized at that level.

MOCKINGBIRD STATION

Dallas, Texas

Development Team

Owner

Real Estate Capital Partners
Herndon, Virginia
www.recp.com

Developer

Hughes Development, LP
Dallas, Texas
www.hughesdevelopment.com

Design Architect

RTKL Associates, Inc.
Los Angeles, California
www.rtkl.com

Architect of Record

Selzer Associates, Inc.
Dallas, Texas
www.selzerarch.com

Landscape Architect

Enviro Design
Dallas, Texas
www.envirodesign-dallas.com

The first mixed-use project designed and built around a multimodal, rail-based transit station in Dallas, Mockingbird Station has achieved what many once thought was impossible: it has convinced middle-class, automobile-driving residents to use transit. The transit-oriented development (TOD)—which contains 178,000 square feet (16,536 m²) of retail, restaurant, and cinema space; 137,000 square feet (12,727 m²) of office space; 211 loft apartments; and parking for 1,580 cars—is immediately adjacent and connected to one of the largest stations on the Dallas Area Rapid Transit (DART) rail line. The station also offers connections to bus, taxi, and shuttle service. Located four miles north of downtown Dallas, the ten-acre (4 ha) project makes use of very dense zoning; its approximately 500,000 square feet (46,450 m²) of rentable building area and 520,000 square feet (48,308 m²) of parking are unprecedented in density outside of Dallas's central business district.

Mockingbird Station combines adaptive use with new construction. Two existing structures—including a historic Western Union telephone assembly building and an office building, which has been expanded—constituted the project's base. The developer, UC Urban (now Hughes Development, LP), made the risky design decision to place the project's "front door" at the rail station platform rather than along the freeway exposure—and to give the project the same name as the station. The result has been that customers and other visitors clearly see how they can get to and from the project by train, and many patrons regularly use DART.

The project's many inventive, cutting-edge features made it difficult for the developer to obtain approvals, infrastructure improvements, financing, and retail tenants. The city was ill prepared to consider the project's unusual traffic and access issues, given its adjacency to transit, while the transit authority was inexperienced in dealing with the needs of developers; construction was thus delayed by several months. Extraordinary efforts were required to obtain both short- and long-term equity and debt funding. The developer had to pay for all road improvements and for the full cost of connecting the project to the rail platform. The developer received no reimbursement from the public sector for assuming these costs, and the project benefited from no special tax districts or permit abatements. The developer was able to obtain—on behalf of the city and the transit agency—federal funding for off-site pedestrian access improvements to the area. Overall, relentless efforts were needed to "sell" the project to government officials, lenders, and prospective retail tenants alike.

As developer Ken Hughes, president of Hughes Development, points out, "When we began this project in the 1990s, there were few real opportunities to make great places around transit stations. Nobody—not the transit agency, nor the development community, nor the city—anticipated Mockingbird Station's emergence as a 'place.' But the developer saw conditions suggesting a great relationship between almost certain rail users and active urban spaces that clearly were possible at the intersection of a freeway, a strong local street system, and the rail station. Mockingbird Station has become a suburban location with the vibrancy, vocabulary, and intimacy of an urban space."

Complete since July 2001, the first phase of Mockingbird Station has proven remarkably successful, particularly since TOD was an untried concept in Texas. Residential occupancies have consistently outpaced the market, with above-average rents for the area. The retail and office space are, respectively, approximately 88 and 92 percent occupied. Future phases are expected to include a hotel and additional retail or residential uses. Mockingbird Station has proved to city, county, and state officials that a properly conceived mixed-use TOD can succeed and flourish by serving the adjacent neighborhood while acting as a catalyst to increase transit use.

Project Data

Project Web Page

www.mockingbirdstation.com

Site Area

ten acres (4 ha)
20 percent open space

Facilities

605,000 square feet (56,206 m²)
gross leasable area

137,000 square feet (12,728 m²)
office area

178,000 square feet (16,537 m²)
retail area

211 rental units

200 surface parking spaces

1,380 structured parking spaces

Land Uses

residential, retail, entertainment, parking

Start/Completion Dates

March 2000–July 2001

NAMBA PARKS

Osaka, Japan

Development Team

Owners/Developers

**Nankai Electric Railway
Company, Ltd.**
Osaka, Japan
www.nankai.co.jp

Takashimaya Company, Ltd.
Osaka, Japan
www.takashimaya.co.jp

Architect

The Jerde Partnership
Venice, California
www.jerde.com

*Architect of Record/
General Contractor*

Obayashi Corporation
Osaka, Japan
www.obayashi.co.jp

Architect (Office Tower)

Nikken Sekkei
Osaka, Japan
www.nikken.co.jp

Landscape Architect

Tsujimoto Ryushouen
Osaka, Japan

Namba Parks is an urban lifestyle center fitted onto a 3.37-hectare (8.33 ac) underused parcel in the heart of Osaka's central business district. The site lies at the northern terminus of railroad land owned by Nankai Electric Railway, which has been developing it over the course of half a century. Surrounded by raised railroad tracks to the east and an urban boulevard and elevated viaduct to the west, Namba Parks created 1.15 hectares (2.8 ac) of green space atop an eight-level assemblage of 108 shops and restaurants, forming an indoor-outdoor urban retail and entertainment complex visually anchored by a 30-floor office tower.

Namba Parks extends the southern edge of Minami, Osaka's historic CBD. It was jointly developed by Nankai and Takashimaya, a prominent department-store chain based in Kyoto, with 24 stores in Japan, Taiwan, Singapore, the United States, and France. Founded in 1885, Nankai is Japan's 16th largest railway company. Like all Japanese railroad companies—indeed, like all large Japanese corporations with landholdings—Nankai has extensive experience with real estate development. Nankai's monopoly on train travel between Osaka and Kansai International Airport brings thousands of travelers to its flagship station at Namba, where they can transfer to Nankai's or others' subways.

In 1957, Nankai and Takashimaya jointly developed the space above Namba station to house Takashimaya's 68,982-square-meter (742,540 sf) store and the 300 shops that make up the retail destination, called Namba City. Adjacent to the block, and connected with it, Nankai built a 36-floor, 548-room hotel, now managed by the Swissôtel chain.

Nankai's and Takashimaya's form of long-term joint venturing is common in Japan, where the *keiretsu* (literal translation: "brotherhood") model of business partnerships is prominent. While Nankai and Takashimaya are not engaged as a *keiretsu*—which by definition involves a merchant-banking relationship—the principles that promote *keiretsus* apply to their partnership. The two firms have access to capital through their separate banking relationships, and with this source of debt financing, guaranteed by their parent companies, the capital to undertake a development like Namba Parks is routinely granted.

In 1997, with Japan still in the midst of a decade-long recession, Nankai began work on the remaining ten hectares (24.7 ac) of the Namba parcel. On this underdeveloped portion was the 21,000-seat Osaka Stadium, home of the major-league Nankai Hawks until 1989. (In 1988, Nankai had sold the Hawks to new owners, who moved the team to Fukuoka.) The ballpark had remained vacant since the team's sale, its infield used as a parking lot and its outfield concourse as the offtrack betting parlors of the Japan Racing Association (JRA). The JRA held an inviolable long-term lease that required Nankai to construct a new 22,000-square-meter (236,806 sf) facility before the stadium could be demolished. Nankai built the new JRA facility on two underground levels and developed Namba Parks around and over it.

Namba Parks' conceptual premise is of a canyon coursing through an urban park. A terraced complex of retail spaces designed by the Jerde Partnership, a Los Angeles–based architecture firm, envelopes an irregular and nonplanar space in the center, open to the sky and flowing out to the entrance. An elevator tower rises in this curvilinear center, and glass-enclosed pedestrian bridges traverse the canyon at various points at different levels, connecting the interior spaces and showcasing pedestrian and shopping traffic. At the uppermost roof level, surrounding the central opening, are outdoor common areas and a terraced amphitheater facing a flat stage area. Cascading from the eighth-level rooftop is a series of green terraces atop the roofs of the retail spaces below, irrigated by recycled graywater filtered from the restaurants within the complex.

Standing at the complex's street-side periphery, the 30-story office tower was sited to cast its extensive shadow most of the day on the adjacent north-south thoroughfare, thus complying with Japan's unique "sun-shadow law" guaranteeing a measure of sunlight to neighboring buildings. Its architect, Nikken Sekkei, designed one of the biggest floor plates in Osaka—measuring about 1,500 square meters (16,146 sf) per floor—using the latest in earthquake-resistant design technology.

The development has increased the ridership entering or exiting Namba station by 9 percent, synergistically drawing record numbers of shoppers to Namba Parks and maintaining more than 90 percent occupancy in the office tower. Construction on the second phase has begun. When completed in 2007, it will extend Namba's canyon, adding 80 shops, some 20,000 square meters (215,275 sf) of retail space, and 0.35 hectares (0.86 ac) of additional rooftop green space. A 344-unit residential tower will stand at the southwest corner, making the completed Namba Parks complex truly mixed use.

Project Data

Web Page

www.nambaparks.com

Site Area

3.37 hectares (8.33 ac)

Facilities

140,000 square meters (1,506,947 sf) gross building area

60,000 square meters (645,835 sf) office area

40,000 square meters (430,556 sf) retail area

363 structured parking spaces

Land Uses

retail, office, entertainment, parking

Start/Completion Dates

1997–October 7, 2003

PRUDENTIAL CENTER REDEVELOPMENT

Boston, Massachusetts

Thirty-five years after it was built, the Prudential Center had an established identity as a large-scale, mixed-use complex of office, retail, hotel, and residential buildings in Boston's Back Bay, the city's second-largest office district, in addition to being the site of Boston's convention center. Yet the "Pru," as it was locally known, had never been able to attract key downtown office tenants, nor had it achieved rent levels comparable to those of downtown buildings. It also was suffering the consequences of a 1960s site plan that walled it off from the surrounding urban streetscape.

Boston Properties acquired the 23-acre (9 ha) property in July 1998, with the goal of expanding and repositioning it as a premier business, residential, and civic address. The firm believed that the success of its plan would depend on a redevelopment that, while adding new buildings, also would change both the reality and the perception of the center's quality, its location, and its relationship to the city. "A primary goal of the redevelopment and expansion of Prudential Center was to link our arcades with the streets and surrounding neighborhoods," says Bryan J. Koop, senior vice president and regional manager for Boston Properties. "Accomplishing this goal has increased our traffic counts by at least 30 percent."

The redevelopment project converted the original center's worst shortcomings into an asset by replacing service roadways at the center's perimeter with new buildings that respect the scale and character of the surrounding neighborhood and are lined with retail storefronts and office and residential building entrances. Completed between 2001 and 2003, the expansion added a 36-story tower with a distinctive crown and 867,000 square feet (80,544 m²) of office space; 132,000 square feet (12,263 m²) of residential condominiums in the upper nine floors of an 11-story building; 149,000 square feet (13,842 m²) of new retail space, including a 57,000-square-foot (5,295 m²) flagship urban supermarket and the city's largest bookstore; a 480-foot-long (146 m) Winter Garden, which completes a glass-roofed pedestrian circulation system open to the public 24/7; a 1.2-acre (0.5 ha) park above below-grade parking; a new handicapped-accessible subway entrance; and a quarter-mile-long (400 m) streetfront that knits the Prudential Center into its urban surroundings with new sidewalks, landscaping, lighting, stores, and street-level entrances.

Like any large-scale urban redevelopment project, the effort faced innumerable challenges. These were complicated by the need to carry out construction immediately adjacent to occupied office, retail, and residential buildings, above a multilevel parking garage and a below-grade turnpike. In response to

Development Team

Owner/Developer

Boston Properties, Inc.
Boston, Massachusetts
www.bostonproperties.com

Architect

CBT/Childs Bertman Tseckares, Inc.
Boston, Massachusetts
www.cbtarchitects.com

Landscape Architects

Carr, Lynch and Sandell, Inc.
Cambridge, Massachusetts
www.carrlynchsandell.com

The Halvorson Company
Boston, Massachusetts
www.halvorsondesign.com

Project Data

Site Area

23 acres (9.3 ha)

Facilities

1,380,400 square feet (128,243 m²) gross building area

1,064,000 square feet (98,849 m²) gross leasable area

867,000 square feet (80,547 m²) office area

149,000 square feet (13,843 m²) retail area

1,320,00 square feet (12,263 m²) residential area

65 residential units

Land Uses

retail, office, residential, hotel (existing)

Start/Completion Dates

2000–April 2003

Jury Statement

The "Pru" returns to prominence with this redevelopment of the 41-year-old landmark. Careful infilling of underused spaces, phased in over two years, has added office, retail, and residential space; public open space; more underground parking; and a new entrance to the MBTA subway. Most of all, the redevelopment of the Prudential Center—once a forbidding island straddling Mass Pike—integrates the 23-acre (9.3 ha) site with its Back Bay neighborhood.

these challenges, Boston Properties established an innovative project management structure, selected a single general contractor for the majority of the project at the start of the design process, and brought in a third-party residential developer for the primarily residential building. Although the project was developed entirely with private funds, it involved extensive public/private interaction and cooperation among groups that included the Prudential Project Advisory Committee, the Boston Redevelopment Authority, the Massachusetts Turnpike Authority, the Massachusetts Bay Transportation Authority, and CSX Transportation.

A resounding economic success, the Prudential Center expansion's office and retail space is 100 percent leased, and its 65 luxury condominiums are sold out. The office tower has attracted tenants from many of the city's top finance, law, and brokerage firms, setting new records for rent levels in the Back Bay. The retail space has attracted high-profile national tenants, and retail sales in 2005 averaged $930 per square foot ($10,011 per m²). The condominiums achieved an average sales price above $800 per square foot ($8,611 per m²) at closing, the highest sales price of any new development in Boston at the time. The project has both expanded and reinvigorated a 41-year-old complex, creating a vibrant place that has fulfilled longstanding city and community goals, created lively new public spaces, reintegrated the complex into the urban fabric, and added new housing and retail uses that enhance and reinforce the area's residential identity.

SOUTHSIDE WORKS

Pittsburgh, Pennsylvania

Development Team

Owner/Developer

Soffer Organization
Pittsburgh, Pennsylvania
www.sofferorganization.com

Public Partner

Urban Redevelopment Authority of
Pittsburgh
Pittsburgh, Pennsylvania
www.ura.org

Master Planners

Development Design Group
Baltimore, Maryland
www.ddg-usa.com

Environmental Planning & Design
Pittsburgh, Pennsylvania
www.epd-pgh.com

Master Planner (original plan)

RTKL
Dallas, Texas
www.rtkl.com

Architects

Davis Gardner Gannon Pope
Architecture
Pittsburgh, Pennsylvania
www.dggp.com

Design 3 Architecture
Pittsburgh, Pennsylvania
www.d3a.com

Graves Architects, Inc.
Pittsburgh, Pennsylvania

After years of sitting idle, a 34-acre (14 ha) parcel that once housed a steel mill on the southern bank of the Monongahela River has been reactivated as a mixed-use urban center that extends an existing business district, rejuvenating Pittsburgh's South Side neighborhood. At buildout, it will contain more than 1 million square feet (92,900 m²) of office space; 445,000 square feet (41,341 m²) of retail space, including a ten-screen cinema; 6.5 acres (2.6 ha) of green space; and 300 condominiums, flats, and loft apartments. Begun in 2000, Phase I of the brownfield redevelopment project known as SouthSide Works is complete. Development on the site continues, and residential condominiums, a hotel and fitness center, and more offices are planned.

After the once-thriving LTV steel mill—the backbone of Pittsburgh's industrial past—closed, its 110-acre (45 ha) site lay vacant until it was claimed by the city's Urban Redevelopment Authority (URA), which then began master-planning studies. After issuing a request for proposals, the URA appointed the Soffer Organization as master developer for almost a third of the site, thus beginning a productive public/private partnership among the authority, the developer, and the city. Plans were reviewed and approved by the community and stakeholders, including the South Side Local Development Company, the city planning department, the South Side Planning Forum, and the LTV Steering Committee. The city was responsible for infrastructure, environmental remediation, and parking, while Soffer was responsible for prior-use remediation. The city used tax increment financing to fund bonds to pay for the infrastructure.

Meeting the overall goal of community revitalization required establishing an uninterrupted flow between existing neighborhoods and the new development. The site is connected to downtown Pittsburgh via the Hot Metal Bridge, an old railroad bridge that the URA renovated for vehicular traffic to support SouthSide Works. Eight major universities—principally the University of Pittsburgh and Carnegie Mellon and Duquesne universities—are located within five miles of the project, which also is accessible by bus. Because of its proximity to these universities, SouthSide Works serves partly as an extension of their campuses, providing valued services to students, staff, and visitors.

The land's previous industrial use presented numerous obstacles to its development. Underground steel-mill foundations discovered during the excavation process had to be cleaned up. A still-functioning rail line tunnels directly under the property, imposing additional constraints: unused spur lines needed to be removed and the land above the railroad, which cannot support a building, was incorporated into the project as green space. The riverfront location and building setback requirements allow for the South Shore Riverfront Park, which is a key link in the city's urban loop, an uninterrupted ten-mile trail system on the shores of the Golden Triangle.

IKM, Inc.
Pittsburgh, Pennsylvania
www.ikminc.com

JSA Architects
Pittsburgh, Pennsylvania
www.jsa-architects.com

TRM Architect
Buffalo, New York
www.trmarchitect.com

WTW Architects
Pittsburgh, Pennsylvania

Project Data

Web Page

www.southsideworks.com

Site Area

34 acres (13.8 ha)

19 percent open green space

Facilities

1 million square feet (92,903 m²) office area

445,000 square feet (41,342 m²) retail area

300 residential units

2,000 structured parking spaces

Land Uses

office, retail, residential, parking, open space

Start Date

2000

After many years of planning, design, and negotiation, the vision of SouthSide Works has been realized. Pittsburgh's universities and companies now use SouthSide Works to recruit knowledge workers and other young professionals who seek an urban experience with in-town residential options, public transportation, entertainment, national and local retailers, and public green space for outdoor activities. Residential and retail rents are exceeding pro forma expectations, and the residential units are 98 percent leased.

Ground breaking for the second phase of development, including a riverfront condominium building and another restaurant, is scheduled to take place in 2006, and a hotel and fitness facility is currently in the design and planning stages. Additional office space also is planned to accommodate expansion by American Eagle Outfitters, the Fortune 500 company that now owns one of the office buildings at South-Side Works. At full buildout, the project will have attracted approximately $350 million in private funding and $75 million in public funding, and will create an estimated additional $7.3 million in annual sales tax as well as 3,000 new jobs.

HOUSING

CHATHAM SQUARE

Alexandria, Virginia

Development Team

Owner/Developer

EYA
Bethesda, Maryland
www.eya.com

Public Partner

Alexandria Redevelopment and
Housing Authority
Alexandria, Virginia
www.alexandriava.gov

Architect

Lessard Group
Vienna, Virginia
www.lessardgroup.com

Landscape Architect

Studio 39 Landscape Architecture, PC
Alexandria, Virginia
www.studio39.com

Few, if any, U.S. communities incorporate both public housing units and market-rate homes that sell for as much as $1 million. A national model for the redevelopment of obsolete public housing led by a market-rate housing provider with minimal government subsidy, Chatham Square does just that, containing 100 market-rate townhomes and 52 public housing units on two city blocks in the historic district of Old Town Alexandria, across the Potomac River from Washington, D.C. An innovative "back-to-back" design of residential units seamlessly integrates new public housing and million-dollar townhomes within the existing neighborhood. It is impossible to distinguish the public housing from the market-rate units, and the architecture of the entire community reflects and blends into the Old Town streetscape.

Plans to redevelop the 100-unit, 4.17-acre (1.7 ha) public housing project began as early as 1989 but met with extensive opposition from residents of both the existing public housing and the surrounding community, and two previous development efforts failed. The site's location within a historic district meant that any plan for its redevelopment had to meet strict architectural guidelines. Developer EYA brought all stakeholders together to resolve longstanding differences and—in partnership with the city of Alexandria, the Alexandria Redevelopment and Housing Authority (ARHA), and Fannie Mae—created a financial and design plan that aimed to achieve each party's goals and improve the neighborhood. The ultimate plan, approved by all stakeholders, features a density of 36 units per acre (89 units/ha) with more than two parking spaces per unit, as well as four large public open spaces with both active and passive recreation areas and more than 100 new street trees. A closed-off through-street was restored, reinforcing the city grid. Public housing units are scattered throughout the site, in buildings that contain four market-rate townhomes on one side and six public rental units that appear to be four townhomes on the other, all above underground parking. Many of the units also feature rooftop terraces. Innovative legal structures and subdivision platting enable fee simple ownership of the townhomes. The project was completed in December 2005. All the townhomes have been sold, at an average cost of $870,000, and all the rental units are occupied.

All parties have benefited financially. The entrepreneurial deal structure, which allowed ARHA to share in the project's financial success, created strong economic incentives for the housing authority to work with the developer in gaining approvals from the city in the most cost- and time-effective manner. EYA purchased the land from ARHA for more than 150 percent of the property's appraised value and tied bonus payments to the appreciated sales value of the market-rate units. ARHA ultimately realized more than $3 million in bonus payments. A percentage of this revenue is being used to fund the construction of additional new public housing units off site. The project was extremely profitable, generating returns

Project Data

Site Area

4.16 acres (1.68 ha)
27 percent (including rooftop decks)
open space

Facilities

316,720 square feet (29,424 m²)
gross building area

152 total residential units: 100 market
rate; 52 affordable

22 surface parking spaces (on site)

272 structured parking spaces
(including townhouse garages)

Land Uses

residential, open space, structured
parking

Start/Completion Dates

February 2004–December 2005

well in excess of industry averages. EYA served as general contractor for the public housing units, which were financed with tax credit equity and the land proceeds.

Chatham Square disproves the common belief that buyers of high-end housing will not purchase homes in mixed-income communities. "Everyone at EYA and ARHA is so proud of the Chatham Square community," notes Robert Youngentob, president of EYA. "It is the result of a public/private partnership that demonstrates high-quality urban planning and architectural design while achieving excellent economic results and tremendous social good." By transforming a public housing project into a denser community with a lower concentration of poverty and seamlessly integrating the design with its surroundings, Chatham Square serves as a model for future mixed-income redevelopment of public housing.

Development Team

Owner/Developer

**CapitaLand Residential Singapore
Pte., Ltd.
Singapore
www.capitalandresidential.com**

Architect

**MKPL Architects
Singapore
www.mkpl.com.sg**

Landscape Architect

**Studio Steed Pte., Ltd.
Singapore
www.icn-design.com**

GLENTREES

Singapore

In the island republic of Singapore, 90 percent of the 4 million population live in apartments. And foreigners may purchase only condominiums—they are barred from owning detached houses. Given this situation, and given the popularity of private outdoor space in multifamily buildings in this tropical nation, it is no wonder that Glentrees has been wildly successful with its offerings of two- to four-bedroom condominiums, each with the option of a small garden, even at the fifth story.

Several drawbacks kept the Glentrees land undeveloped, despite being situated in the Mount Sinai neighborhood, known for estate homes, proximity to shopping, and other convenient amenities. The undersized infill site is shaped like a lopsided bow tie; it was zoned for a maximum of five stories; it had an open drainage ditch running through its center; and it was landlocked. It had no street frontage, save for a driveway easement just wide enough for two lanes of traffic to the nearest street. Furthermore, the decision to redevelop CapitaLand's 999-year leasehold was made in 2002 in the midst of an economic slowdown, when demand was weak and purchase prices were trending downward.

Bordered by a public elementary school on one side, railroad tracks on another, and taller residential high rises nearby, the site offered no views to enhance. Thus, the condominiums line the perimeter, facing inward toward an irregularly shaped 50-meter (164 ft) lap pool in a common garden. By turning their backs to the site boundaries, the private spaces are shaded by trees along a green buffer zone, while the living spaces are open to the garden view and feature abundant natural light. All the condominiums are through units, and cross-ventilation helps cool them. The drainage ditch was attractively reconfigured as a water garden, integrated within the overall landscape scheme.

All units have private underground parking, and glass-faced elevators rise from the garage level, allowing full view of the central garden. They range from two to four bedrooms on one to three levels, 125 to 341 square kilometers (1,345 to 3,670 sf). While apartments with upper-level balconies and terraces are commonplace, they have typically been surfaced with tiles, with just enough space for chairs and potted plants. Glentrees was the first condominium development in Singapore to offer plantable gardens, up to ten square meters (108 sf) for each unit. They overlook the complex's center, terracing back from the first to the fifth level, opening up the common garden even more to the sky. At the time of first purchase, buyers were offered the option of converting their garden space to a pond, a lawn, or a wooden deck.

In the first year of sales, after November 2002, 57 percent of the units were sold at an average of s$7,912 per square meter (us$417 per sf). By the time all units were constructed, in May 2005, 20 percent remained unsold; today, it is sold out in a still soft market. The current prevailing price in the high-end submarket is s$7,600 per square meter (us$424 per sf); Glentrees is commanding s$8,234 (us$459).

Project Data

Web Page

www.capitalandresidential.com

Site Area

2.1 hectares (5.1 ac)

60 percent open space

Facilities

28,883 square meters (310,894 sf) gross building area

176 residential units

248 structured parking spaces

Land Uses

residential, parking, open space

Start/Completion Dates

February 2003–May 2005

Jury Statement

In land-scarce Singapore, this five-story, 176-unit condominium complex provides residents with their own plantable garden terraces. Situated on a landlocked two-hectare (4.9 ac) infill site with challenging zoning and topographical constraints, the units, each with a view of a central garden, offer a residential environment of unexpectedly high quality.

MISSION MERIDIAN VILLAGE

South Pasadena, California

Development Team

Owners/Developers

Creative Housing Associates
Los Angeles, California
www.challc.com

Lambert Development, LLC
Pacific Palisades, California
www.lambertdevelopment.com

Owner (Parking)

City of South Pasadena
Pasadena, California
www.ci.pasadena.ca.us

Architect

Moule & Polyzoides
Pasadena, California
www.mparchitects.com

Public Partners

State of California

**Los Angeles County Metropolitan
Transit Authority**

City of South Pasadena

Located between a traditional residential neighborhood of single-family homes and a recently revitalized historic neighborhood's commercial center, Mission Meridian Village is the largest infill project ever built within the city of South Pasadena, California. This development around transit contains 67 housing units and 5,000 square feet (465 m²) of retail space set atop a two-level, 324-space subterranean parking garage on a 1.6-acre (0.7 ha) site.

The project's success is attributable in part to a "blended density" approach, in which higher-density development is positioned near a commercial street and density decreases as one approaches the adjacent single-family neighborhood. Fourteen residential lofts are located in a structure that is similar in design and scale to a neighboring commercial building built in the late 1800s, while lower-density duplex homes are contained within structures similar to the single-family bungalows across the street. The result is a density that ranges from 16 to 80 units per acre (40 to 198 per ha), for an overall average density of 40 units per acre (99 per ha).

The project resulted from an innovative public/private partnership. "Mission Meridian Village is evidence of what can happen when the public and private sectors work together," states Michael L. Dieden, president of Creative Housing Associates. "The partnership that the private development entity (Creative Housing Associates, Lambert Development, and Wells Fargo Bank Capital Markets Group) formed with the city of South Pasadena, the Los Angeles County Metropolitan Transit Authority (MTA), and the California Department of Transportation (Caltrans) proved to be the glue that made this remarkable mixed-use, transit-oriented project possible. The lessons we learned from this positive experience are now helping us replicate this coalition as we work with other cities and transit authorities."

Public participation in the project stemmed from a need to provide commuter parking to support the Metro Gold Line's Mission Street rail transit station. The city's initiation of eminent domain proceedings allowed for the assemblage of much of the property. The remainder of the mostly vacant land was owned by an adjacent convalescent hospital and contained two historic bungalows—one of which was used as the hospital laundry, the other as a rental house—as well as employee parking. The developer's purchase agreement with the hospital included providing replacement parking and new laundry facilities. The developer also worked with the city, Caltrans, and Pasadena Heritage to relocate the bungalows (to a site owned by Caltrans), restore them, and sell them to first-time homebuyers.

The MTA granted the city $2.56 million in public transportation funds for construction of the garage; Caltrans provided an additional $1.5 million for the garage and utility relocation, and the city contributed $500,000; the total public contribution was $5 million, or approximately 20 percent of the project's $25 million total cost. All parties functioned as partners throughout the design, entitlement, construction, and operation phases. The use of public funds for the parking structure required an extensive negotiation period with various public agencies, culminating in a series of agreements to ensure the dedication of the structure's second level for public uses. The parking structure's uses thus are completely segregated by level, with separate entrances (one for residents and another for the public) and no vertical connection—for either cars or pedestrians—between the two levels.

Mission Meridian Village is a classic example of a development-around-transit project built within a challenging infill site. A creative design by Moule & Polyzoides Architects (two of the founders of the Congress for New Urbanism) that responds to and reflects its surroundings made it possible to build a high-density project within a historic single-family residential neighborhood. Mission Meridian Village provides much-needed housing and a public parking facility that supports the Mission Street transit station and local businesses in a way that is sensitive to the community's distinctive built environment.

Project Data

Site Area

1.6 acres (6,474 m²)

Facilities

212,094 square feet (19,704 m²) gross building area

5,000 square feet (466 m²) retail area

67 residential units

324 underground parking spaces

Land Uses

residential, retail, parking

Start/Completion Dates

December 2001–January 2005

RADIO CITY

Toronto, Ontario, Canada

Development Team

Owner/Developer

Context Development, Inc.
Toronto, Ontario, Canada
www.context.ca

Architect

Architects Alliance
Toronto, Ontario, Canada
www.architectsalliance.com

Interior Design

Hudson Kruse Design
Toronto, Ontario, Canada
www.hudsonkruse.com

Landscape Architect

Corban and Goode
Toronto, Ontario, Canada

After the Canadian Broadcast Corporation (CBC) moved its English-language broadcasting headquarters from this historic Toronto neighborhood in 1997, the land and buildings sat vacant for several years. Context Development, Inc., later purchased the 2.4-acre (1.0 ha) site and, in conjunction with the National Ballet School of Canada (NBS), structured a deal that allowed the NBS to purchase roughly half the land—on which it would restore two historic buildings and construct a new school—for the nominal fee of $1. The city then granted Context Development the density transfers it needed for financially feasible development of 18 townhouses and two high-rise condominium towers with underground garages on the remaining half of the site. The result is an innovative, high-density, urban infill residential project connected to a new, state-of-the-art NBS complex via two landscaped courtyards. The project's name, Radio City, reflects the CBC's historic presence and evokes images of New York City's Radio City Music Hall.

According to Howard Cohen, president of Context Development, "Radio City was an exciting opportunity to help transform a decrepit piece of land in Toronto's downtown core into a vibrant, mixed-use project. The success of Radio City lies in that it has provided much-needed residential density alongside a new home for the National Ballet School of Canada."

Most of Radio City's residential units (414) are located in two slender high-rise towers—the 25-story North Tower and the 30-story South Tower. The structures' unusually small floor plates—650 square meters (6,997 sf)—and their placement, set back from the street edge, minimize their apparent bulk and do not disturb the residential scale of surrounding side streets, while the condominiums range from studios to units with two bedrooms and a den to penthouses. The three-story townhouses echo the rooflines and form of the adjacent Victorian rowhouses. The arrangement of the buildings creates an interior court that serves as an "address" for the project, while a pair of linked courtyards connects it to the NBS complex. The structures' modern architecture relates to but does not mimic the neighborhood's existing buildings.

Like many urban infill developments, the project ran into a major roadblock along the way to completion. During the excavation process, an underground river was discovered directly below the site of the North Tower. Dewatering took six months, and a portion of the underground parking garage was eliminated from the plans in order to avoid any environmental impact on the river system.

Radio City is located in the Church/Wellesley Village, home to one of Toronto's densest rental markets. The project responds to pent-up demand for for-sale housing from the area's hip, upwardly mobile residents. Because the village also is the heart of Toronto's gay community, Context geared its marketing efforts almost exclusively to these prospective homebuyers, and more than 90 percent of Radio City purchasers ultimately came from this demographic group.

Launched in May 2001 and substantially completed in January 2005, the $85 million (Canadian) project is a clear financial success. Both towers sold out quickly, and resale values continue to climb, outperforming most of the surrounding market. Overall, Radio City has benefited the community greatly, both by introducing new housing that replaced vacant land and empty buildings and by enabling the NBS to construct a new school in conjunction with the restoration of historic structures.

Project Data

Web Page

www.context.ca/pages/radiocity/
radiocity_main.htm

Site Area

1.2 acres (0.5 ha)

Facilities

350,000 square feet (32,515 m²)
gross building area

432 total residential units:
414 condominiums, 18 townhouses

Land Uses

residential

Start/Completion Dates

May 2001–January 2005

PLANNED
COMMUNITY

BEACON COVE

Port Melbourne, Australia

Development Team

Developer

Mirvac Group (Victoria)
Melbourne, Australia
www.mirvac.com.au

Public Partner

Major Projects Victoria
Melbourne, Australia
www.majorprojects.vic.gov.au

Architect and Town Planner

HPA Pty., Ltd.
Melbourne, Australia
www.mirvac.com.au/hpa

Landscape Architect

MDG Landscape Architects
Albert Park, Australia
www.mdgla.com.au

The historic waterfront of Port Melbourne, once a thriving docklands, has been transformed into Beacon Cove, a new community that takes advantage of the site's industrial heritage and its dramatic vista of Port Phillip Bay. Four kilometers (2.5 mi) southwest of downtown Melbourne, Beacon Cove is a public/private master-planned community marketed to young professionals who want the benefits of close-in living, including an easy commute to work.

Developed by Mirvac in a joint venture with the Victoria state government's Major Projects Victoria, the 32-hectare (79 ac) site has been built out over a ten-year period between 1996 and 2006, with a total of 1,517 residential units and 4.5 hectares (11 ac) of open common space and recreational amenities. The design team worked to integrate the new construction within the existing inland suburban neighborhood, while emphasizing the site's harbor-front roots. A diverse range of housing types and densities, designed by Mirvac's in-house planning and design team, HPA Pty., Ltd., is organized according to a pedestrian-oriented plan with a three-acre (one ha) town center and a generous promenade along the bay.

Long after the port's days as a shipping center ended and after its short second life as a petroleum depot, the state of Victoria remediated a large swath of Port Melbourne for redevelopment in the 1980s. After a failed attempt by a private developer to build a mixed-use complex of office towers and housing, the state government stepped in, inviting community residents to take part in a design charrette in 1992. With design goals influenced by community input, the Victorian government issued a detailed call for proposals, resulting in a joint initiative with Mirvac that became Beacon Cove.

Port Melbourne is not only the site of Melbourne's first seaport and the country's first steam railroad, built in 1854, but it also possesses two of the largest timber-piled wharf structures in the Southern Hemisphere. With such historic riches, preservation and restoration efforts were important to longtime residents—and they became a marketable asset for Beacon Cove.

Among the maritime structures preserved by the developers are the Port Melbourne Channel Lights, two historic concrete lighthouses constructed in 1924. One of them, at the far end of Beacon Cove, is still in operation, its flashing lights visible from 37 kilometers (20 nautical miles). Both beacons have been restored, giving the community its name, and a new boulevard, Beacon Vista, which serves as a main artery in the master plan, establishes a view corridor between the two lighthouses.

Beacon Cove's developers and planners designed a vibrant public realm, with a large percentage of parks and open spaces and a commercial district known as Civic Square. Adjacent to Princes Pier, one of the bay's original piers, the square is occupied by a child-care center, a gymnasium, a sports and recreation center, a medical center, neighborhood grocery and convenience store, waterfront restaurants, and

cafés. The square is a transportation hub, with a light-rail station for commuters; the restored Port Melbourne railway station, its terminal on nearby Station Pier serving Victoria's trans-Tasman lines; local ferries; and international passenger cruise ships. The square also is a civic nexus from which a promenade, a network of public parks, public beaches, and open spaces emanate. Directly linked to the promenade, Civic Square is surrounded by high-density residential buildings to maximize patronage for shops, restaurants, and other commercial amenities.

Phase I of development, completed and fully occupied within four years, consists of 478 attached, detached, and semiattached housing units and 467 condominiums in four waterfront apartment towers; three-story townhouses with home offices; and low-rise apartment buildings. In 2002, Civic Square got its light-rail station, providing service to Melbourne and its suburbs. The first stage also included construction of the 457-meter-long (1,500 ft) promenade that connects the port's two large piers, Station and Princes Piers, as well as Sandridge, a public beach restored as part of the development agreement between Mirvac and the state government.

The orientation, height, and density of the residential structures give primacy to water views. The plan positions the tallest buildings—four large apartment towers between ten and 13 stories, with their longest sides facing the bay—along the waterfront promenade, with a gradual reduction in height and density further inland. Three- and four-story terrace home office–style units occupy the inland side of the towers, providing a transition between the high rises near the water to the south and the low-rise housing areas to the north.

Low-rise units come in several different configurations and sizes, from large, semidetached homes and paired courtyard houses to single-story courtyard homes. Many of the units in the low-rise residential buildings have large, open-plan rooms on the ground floor, suitable for use as home offices, and living spaces on the second floor with terraces and balconies. Staggered building lines and strategic placement of windows, balconies, and terraces maximize views to the bay and the lighthouses.

Project Data

Web Page

www.mirvac.com.au/forsale/VIC/
beaconcove_new

Site Area

32 hectares (79 ac)

14 percent open public space

Facilities

**4,000 square meters (43,056 sf)
retail area**

**945 total residential units:
467 apartments, 478 houses**

**800 structured, 860 surface parking
spaces**

Land Uses

**residential, retail, office, transportation,
recreation, open space**

Start/Completion Dates

1996–2006

JINJI LAKE WATERFRONT

Suzhou, China

Development Team

Owner/Developer

**Suzhou Industrial Park
Administrative Committee
Suzhou, China
www.sipac.gov.cn**

*Master Planner/
Landscape Architect*

**EDAW, Ltd.
Hong Kong, China
www.edaw.com**

Site Engineer

**Suzhou Industrial Park Design and
Research Institute Company, Ltd.
Suzhou, China**

The Jinji Lake Waterfront district is the centerpiece of the Suzhou Industrial Park (SIP), a "special economic zone" surrounding Jinji Lake that is being developed as a large-scale planned community. For the new community of 600,000 residents, Jinji Lake will be a visual focus and provide an identity and organizing framework for the SIP's recreational resources and its economic and environmental sustainability.

In 1994, the Chinese government designated the 2,300-hectare (5,683 ac) area, four kilometers (2.5 miles) east of the ancient city of Suzhou (population 5 million), as one of 14 special economic zones where foreign investment is encouraged. Developed as a joint venture between the governments of China and Singapore, the SIP is projected to generate 360,000 new jobs by its full buildout in 2020. After almost a decade of false starts and negotiations among the two national governments and the city of Suzhou and prospective private partners, the Hong Kong office of landscape architect and environmental planner EDAW, Ltd., was commissioned to design the new community's interface with the 740-hectare (1,829 ac) Jinji Lake, the most prominent natural landscape feature in the SIP. Drawing on the two famed identities of Suzhou—its canals and walled gardens—EDAW conceptualized the district as eight neighborhoods with diverse water and landscape expressions encircling Jinji Lake.

Each neighborhood has its own identity. Neighborhoods on the western and northern shores, closer to the city of Suzhou, feature broad promenades that attract residents and workers to the water's edge. Waterfront parks are adjacent to shopping, entertainment, and cultural destinations. These neighborhoods have names like Cityside Harbor, Marina Cove, Grand Promenade, and Arts and Entertainment Village. On the eastern and southern shores, farther from Suzhou, lie lakefront destinations for more pas-

sive recreation and environmental education; these neighborhoods are poetically named Reflection Point, Discovered Island, Mirror's Crossing, and Reflection Gardens.

All the neighborhoods are connected by a continuous walkway along the 14.5-kilometer (nine mi) perimeter of the lake. A variety of hard and soft water edges, created and natural wetlands, and green spaces work together to clean surface water and filter pollutants in agricultural and stormwater runoff. A two-kilometer-long (1.2 mi) vehicular and pedestrian bridge across a bay at the lake's northern end will symbolize the transition from the old to the new Suzhou as the community grows around Jinji Lake and the center of gravity moves eastward from the old city. As more neighborhoods are constructed—three are now complete—Jinji Lake Waterfront will fulfill its master plan as a new town, an economic generator, and a template for environmental sustainability.

The Suzhou Industrial Park was modeled after Jurong Town, an industrial district in Singapore that the former prime minister of China, Deng Xiaoping, visited in 1992, prompting him to invite the country to help the Chinese in establishing a truly global enterprise zone. Though Singapore has retreated to a minority role in the SIP, and the Suzhou region hosts a competing industrial park, the SIP continues to showcase Sino-Singapore cooperation and the global economy, attracting over US$20 billion in contractual investment from 1,888 foreign companies. The Jinji Lake Waterfront project has enhanced the SIP's overall success by adding a recreational and environmental dimension to Suzhou. Already, land values in the waterfront district have increased fourfold, and 2 million visitors from outside Suzhou came to Jinji Lake in 2005.

Project Data

Web Page

www.suzhou.gov.cn

Site Area

515 hectares (1,273 ac)

Facilities

public-use infrastructure, open space, recreational, cultural, educational, residential, entertainment, commercial (at buildout)

Land Use

open space

Start Date

1998

LADERA RANCH

Orange County, California

Development Team

Owners/Developers

Rancho Mission Viejo
San Juan Capistrano, California
www.RanchomissionViejo.com

DMB Consolidated Holdings, LLC
Scottsdale, Arizona
www.dmbinc.com

Master Planner

EDAW, Inc.
Irvine, California
www.edaw.com

Architect

William Hezmalhalch Architects, Inc.
Santa Ana, California
www.whainc.com

Landscape Architect

Land Concern, Ltd.
Santa Ana, California
www.landconcern.com

Civil Engineer

Huitt Zollars, Inc.
Irvine, California
www.huitt-zollars.com

A scenic, view-oriented, environmentally responsible community that strikes a careful balance between preserving natural resources and providing much-needed housing, Ladera Ranch, which was begun in 1998 and substantially completed in 2006, is a 4,000-acre (1,619 ha) master-planned community carved out of southern California's vast Rancho Mission Viejo. More than 1,600 acres (648 ha) of sensitive habitat are being preserved as open space under a perpetual land trust, leaving about 2,400 acres (971 ha) to be developed with 8,100 homes and 1 million square feet (92,900 m²) of commercial space in six villages and three multiuse districts, with a relatively high average density—for production housing on a greenfield site—of 7.1 units per acre (17.5/ha). A central biofiltration system collects and naturally treats low-flow stormwater runoff, while a centralized computer system tightly controls irrigation, reducing water use. The community's final two villages, Terramor and Covenant Hills, have incorporated a wide range of pioneering green building techniques, making Ladera Ranch one of the largest concentrations of green-designed and -constructed homes in the United States and the nation's largest solar community.

Reflecting the theme of "neighborhood as amenity," Ladera Ranch is organized around a hierarchy of community, village, and neighborhood planning goals. Its soft infrastructure and governance structures are among the most ambitious and sophisticated in the nation. These elements—which include a communitywide intranet that links residents, local businesses, and social, civic, and recreational activities—have nurtured hundreds of groups, clubs, and events, resulting in a clear sense of community. Each of Ladera Ranch's villages has its own identity, which takes design cues from historical southern California building types; most important, the project makes a strong break with the region's 25-year reliance on stucco and tile as the predominant palette of materials. Villages vary subtly in street pattern, density, landscape, architecture, and lifestyle. Detailed design guidelines help balance the charm and appeal of traditional neighborhood design with the unforgiving demands of high-volume production home-builders. "One of the development team's most significant accomplishments," notes Marc Lamkin, director of community development for Rancho Mission Viejo, "was the ability to bring approximately 1,000 residential lots to the builder market each year."

Each 900- to 1,400-home village contains a core comprising a village club as well as other public facilities that may include a child care center, school, library, and village green. To optimize sales and create a diverse community, each village also contains a wide range of housing types at a variety of price points, including rental apartments, stacked condominiums, townhomes, and live/work units, as well as single-family products ranging from houses on conventional lots to garden and motor courts, and alley-loaded, custom, and semicustom home lots. To avoid a sense of separation between the villages, a four-mile-long

(6 km) promenade, open space, and activity corridor links residents with community facilities in their own and other villages. At the neighborhood level, all homes are located within two blocks of a neighborhood park or open space, and design guidelines specify architectural treatments for homes on corners, street trees, roundabouts, sidewalks separated from the street by planting strips, and other elements to ensure diverse, attractive, walkable neighborhoods. By shifting the focus of design and planning back to the neighborhood level, Ladera Ranch has demonstrated that authentic, diverse, well-thought-out neighborhoods can increase both sales and land and home values.

Project Data

Web Page

www.laderaranch.com

Site Area

4,000 acres (1,619 ha)

Facilities

1 million square feet (92,903 m²)
commercial and retail space

5,000 square feet (465 m²) retail space

8,100 residential units

Land Uses

residential, recreational, office, retail,
conservation

Start/Completion Dates

1998–2006

Jury Statement

Started in 1998, Ladera Ranch is a
4,000-acre (1,619 ha), 8,100-unit new
community carved out of southern
California's vast Rancho Mission Viejo.
Forty percent of its land area is preserved as open space, and the balance
has been developed creatively in a
variety of self-contained neighborhoods, one of which leads the nation in
residential solar-powered homes. By
employing best practices in planning
and environmental management,
this new community has brought about
significant economic results for the
developer, the homebuyers, and the
region.

The community has been a grand-slam economic success for its developers, Rancho Mission Viejo and DMB Consolidated Holdings, LLC, achieving an internal rate of return of more than 50 percent. Ladera Ranch has raised the bar and set a new standard for the development of master-planned communities in southern California. Its final villages also have created a breakthrough model for sustainable, green-building practices; multiple national production builders that had never before taken on green-building projects are applying these techniques to various projects elsewhere.

PORT CREDIT VILLAGE

Mississauga, Ontario, Canada

Development Team

Owners/Developers

FRAM Building Group
Mississauga, Ontario, Canada
www.framhomes.com

Slokker Canada
Vienna, Virginia
www.slokker.us

Architect

Giannone Associates
Toronto, Canada
www.giannoneassociates.com

Landscape Architects

Baker Turner Landscape Architects
Brampton, Ontario, Canada
www.bakerturner.com

John George Associates
Burlington, Ontario, Canada

Planner

Korsiak and Company
Oakville, Ontario, Canada

Port Credit Village has reclaimed an underused industrial site on Lake Ontario, 20 minutes west of downtown Toronto, and transformed it into an appealing mixed-use, mixed-income town center. The project joins two formerly separated sides of Port Credit, a village with a 170-year history, connecting it with a restored waterfront and providing a transition area between high-rise development on the west and single-family housing on the east.

Formerly occupied by the St. Lawrence Starch Company—a major corporate citizen that once employed most of village's citizens—the 26-acre (10.5 ha) brownfield site was contaminated with industrial waste that had to be remediated before development could take place. In 1998, the FRAM Building Group and Slokker Canada saw an opportunity to redevelop the site as a mixed-used project that would create new urban experiences for Port Credit residents as well as reestablish important links to the existing urban fabric and the waterfront. Residents, having battled earlier high-density developments, were wary of the impact this project would have on their community. FRAM/Slokker took their concerns to heart, modifying earlier, inherited plans after numerous meetings with local stakeholders, and the result was a proposal for a medium-density project that met with widespread community support. This collaborative approach effectively helped fast-track the development through the approvals process.

Completed in 2005, Port Credit Village contains 410 residential units, 40,000 square feet (3,716 m²) of commercial (retail and office) space, 18 live/work units, and nearly 600 parking spaces. Located just blocks from a commuter rail station, it complements the province's smart growth initiative by intensifying pedestrian-oriented suburban development along a major transportation corridor. To maintain the project's "pedestrians first" feel, most of the parking is located underground. This also frees up ground-level space for vibrant, people-oriented places such as parks and public squares. The live/work units, set in two buildings that respect the typical small-town streetscape, create a distinctive lifestyle opportunity for residents to live above high-end retail shops and service establishments. Industrial artifacts from the starch factory as well as the company's old administration building have been preserved as reminders of the site's industrial heritage. The redesigned and reconstructed shoreline, as well as new shoals constructed in the bay, reduce wave uprush and create habitat for native aquatic species.

FRAM/Slokker's goal at Port Credit Village was to create a community in which people could live, work, and relax within walking distance of their favorite amenities. It also aimed to bring together the

Project Data

Web Page

www.portcreditvillage.com

Site Area

26 acres (10.5 ha)

17 percent common open space

Facilities

**40,000 square feet (3,716 m²)
retail area**

410 residential units

596 structured parking spaces

Land Uses

retail, residential, parking

Start/Completion Dates

1998–2005

two sides of Port Credit, connecting the village's commercial strip with the waterfront and the rest of the community. It establishes a connection to the water by creating views and public spaces along the water's edge, and it provides a variety of public spaces that encourage all types of activity, from quiet strolls to large, festive gatherings. Its residences are almost completely sold out, and the commercial space is 100 percent leased, at more than double the area's average rental rates when the project began. Retail lease rates in the immediate area have risen as well.

The project clearly has revitalized Mississauga, not only by building and increasing density, but also by making the community more user-friendly and by serving as a catalyst for further development. As Frank Giannone, president of FRAM Building Group, notes, "We are proud of how our Port Credit Village project has become a catalyst for the revitalization of the city of Mississauga's waterfront. Our commitment to a process of open dialogue with both the community and authorities has taken an inherited 'hornet's nest' of distrust in the development process and achieved unprecedented support. The innovative urban design solutions, careful mix of residential types, and other commercial and public uses married to award-winning architecture and landscape architecture have set a new standard for mixed-use brownfield and infill developments in the greater Toronto area."

THE PRESIDIO TRUST MANAGEMENT PLAN

San Francisco, California

The Presidio's transformation from U.S. Army post to national park began in 1972, when Congress created the Golden Gate National Recreation Area, a vast network of contiguous historic sites and preserved open space along the San Francisco Bay coast, mandating that the Presidio—the nation's oldest military post—would become part of this area when it was no longer needed by the military. In 1994, the army lowered its flag there for the last time, and the Presidio was transferred to the U.S. National Park Service. Anchoring the San Francisco side of the Golden Gate Bridge, the 1,500-acre (607 ha) site contains the infrastructure of a small city as well as expansive open space, a 300-acre (121 ha) historic forest, spectacular views, and rare and endangered plants and wildlife. It comprises nearly 6 million square feet (557,400 m²) of buildings, including 469 historic structures that contribute to its status as a National Historic Landmark District, making it unlike any other national park.

Recognizing the unprecedented challenges and costs involved in managing such a complex place, in 1996 Congress created a federal government corporation known as the Presidio Trust to preserve the Presidio as an enduring resource for the American people, and provided for an annually diminishing appropriation until 2013, when the Trust is expected to become self-sufficient. The Presidio Trust Management Plan, completed in May 2002, sets the framework for the Presidio's financial and preservation goals.

"Guiding the Presidio into its new life as a national park is a tremendous responsibility," says Craig Middleton, executive director of the Presidio Trust. "Congress has asked us to protect the Presidio's incomparable resources, provide for its ongoing financial sustainability, and create new opportunities for the public to experience the post as a park. This mission calls for us to reach for excellence and to look for innovative ways of blending private and public resources to accomplish a public purpose. It is the opportunity of a lifetime."

The Presidio Trust Management Plan already has taken the Presidio quite far along the road to self-sufficiency. The Trust has attracted more than $400 million in private capital, and about 1.8 million square feet (167,220 m²) of nonresidential buildings have been rehabilitated and leased to a dynamic mix of nonprofit, for-profit, and government organizations. Approximately 4,000 people work in the park, and its 1,100 rehabilitated residences are now 97 percent occupied. In FY 2004 and 2005, the Trust's earned revenue—which reached more than $50 million in 2005—exceeded the cost of operations. The Trust expects to complete key capital upgrades within the next ten years.

Development Team

Owner/Developer

The Presidio Trust
San Francisco, California
www.presidiotrust.gov

Planner

Sasaki Associates, Inc.
Watertown, Massachusetts
www.sasaki.com

Project Data

Web Page

www.presidiotrust.gov

Site Area

1,500 acres (607 ha)

Facilities

5,960,000 square feet (553,702 m²)
gross building area
1,100 residential units

Land Uses

residential, public open spaces,
recreational, educational, cultural,
retail, office

Start Date

June 2000

Jury Statement

The Presidio Trust was enacted by Congress to preserve the Presidio—once a military post with the infrastructure of a small town—as a 1,168-acre (473 ha) national park and treasured landmark for all people for all time. Its management plan, projected to make the Presidio financially self-sufficient by 2013, is a model for balancing economic and preservation goals, as well as private and public interests.

At buildout, capital costs for the Presidio will exceed $600 million. Annual operating expenses are expected to stabilize at $43 million per year, making it the most expensive national park to operate and maintain. By keeping its plans flexible and responding to changing market conditions, the Trust is balancing its park preservation and financial goals, enabling it to continue to rehabilitate buildings, restore natural resources, expand open space, and preserve the Presidio's historic character.

The Presidio is thus being reborn as a new community in the midst of one of San Francisco's most cherished open spaces. Unlike the wildlands of most national parks, the Presidio is a place where everyday human pursuits keep the spirit and history of the place alive, where diverse activities blend into a broader civic context, and where government agencies and private organizations and businesses work together to benefit the public good. The Presidio Trust Management Plan offers a model planning strategy for other closed and closing military bases elsewhere in the United States and throughout the world.

STAPLETON DISTRICT 1

Denver, Colorado

From 1929 through 1995, Stapleton International Airport served as Denver's municipal airport. By 1987, plans were underway to build a new, state-of-the-art airport farther east, and they met voter approval in 1989. Meanwhile, a nonprofit group of civic and business leaders, working in partnership with the city of Denver, formed the Stapleton Development Foundation to determine the disposition of the soon-to-be-redundant Stapleton airport. In 1999, based on the foundation's guidelines for development, the city selected Forest City Enterprises to be the master developer of the publicly owned site—located just five miles from downtown—which offered the largest urban redevelopment opportunity in Denver's history. Today, the former airport is being reborn as a 4,700-acre (1,902 ha) master-planned community that, at buildout, will contain more than 12,000 homes, 13 million square feet (1.2 million m²) of commercial development, and more than 1,100 acres (445 ha) of parks and open space. Construction began in 2001, and the first phase, Stapleton District 1, was substantially complete in 2005. Encompassing 489 acres (198 ha), District 1 contains 2,100 residences—ranging from rental apartments to single-family homes, in many styles and price ranges—plus 200,000 square feet (18,580 m²) of office and industrial space, 120,000 square feet (11,148 m²) of retail space, more than 100 acres (40 ha) of parks and open space, and four schools. Reversing the traditional "retail follows rooftops" approach, Forest City built two retail centers in the project's first year. Although the community is only 25 percent complete, District 1 already offers a mature, walkable, mixed-use community that is home to 4,500 residents.

Conceived as a sustainable, pedestrian-oriented, urban infill community with an average residential density of more than ten units per acre (25 units per ha), Stapleton's development is being guided by a new urbanist development plan that outlines not only the community vision for the built environment but also addresses important social goals related to education, affordable housing, demographic diversity, and more; by a sustainability master plan that requires all housing to meet or exceed Colorado's Built Green and federal Energy Star standards; and by a 130-page design book that aims to give the community a distinctive look and feel, with a wide variety of architecture and product types informed by the historic neighborhoods of Denver. Nearly 30 percent of District 1 has been dedicated to parks and open space; when complete, Stapleton will increase Denver's city park acreage by nearly 30 percent. "It's a rare real estate opportunity that allows us to create a community where walkability, sustainability, education, and open space all coexist with such ease," comments Hank Baker, senior vice president of Forest City Stapleton, Inc. "Denver's far-reaching community vision for Stapleton and Forest City's generational perspective to development have combined to create a magical community that will endure for generations to come."

Development Team

Owner/Developer

Forest City Enterprises
Denver, Colorado
www.stapletondenver.com

Planners

Calthorpe Associates
Berkeley, California
www.calthorpe.com

EDAW, Inc.
Denver, Colorado
www.edaw.com

Site Engineers

URS Corporation
Denver, Colorado
www.urscorp.com

Matrix Design Group
Denver, Colorado
www.matrixdesigngroup.com

Architect

4240 Architecture, Inc.
Denver, Colorado
www.4240arch.com

Project Data

Web Page

www.StapletonDenver.com

Site Area

489 acres (198 ha), District 1

20 percent common open space

Facilities

200,000 square feet (18,581 m²) office area

120,000 square feet (11,148 m²) retail area

2,100 residential units

1,000 surface parking spaces

150 structured parking spaces

Land Uses

residential, retail, office, civic, cultural

Start/Completion Dates

2001–2005 (District 1)

Jury Statement

When completed, the Stapleton project will have transformed Denver's former municipal airport into a 4,700-acre (1,902 ha), master-planned community that meshes seamlessly with its urban surroundings. At this still-early stage, a 489-acre (198 ha) new neighborhood for 2,100 households has been completed successfully, proving the viability of the concept.

Forest City contracted to buy 2,935 developable acres (1,195 ha) in three phases—at least 1,000 acres (405 ha) every five years—for $79.4 million, increased annually by the consumer price index, plus an additional $15,000 per acre ($37,066 per ha) for open-space conservation. Tax increment financing is being used to underwrite infrastructure costs such as streets, parks, and schools. The community is already a clear financial success: housing demand exceeds availability, land and home prices are escalating, and the retail and office space is substantially leased. Stapleton has become a national model. It demonstrates that large-scale urban redevelopment can compete with suburban greenfield development; that a mix of uses can be successfully included early in the life of a new community; that both the image and the reality of urban public schools can be improved in ways that benefit the community and create a market advantage; that traditional neighborhood design need not be limited to traditional architectural forms; and that mixed-income housing can be accepted by the market and does not deter appreciation.

VARSITY LAKES

Gold Coast City, Queensland, Australia

Development Team

Owner/Developer

Delfin Lend Lease
Varsity Lakes, Queensland, Australia
www.delfinlendlease.com.au

Architects

Dryhurst Halstead Stuart
Gold Coast City, Queensland, Australia

Alan Griffith Architects
Gold Coast City, Queensland, Australia

Design Forum Architects
Gold Coast City, Queensland, Australia

Hamilton Hayes Henderson
Gold Coast City, Queensland, Australia

Design Engineers

Baseline
Gold Coast City, Queensland, Australia

Brad Lees Consulting
Gold Coast City, Queensland, Australia

Cozens Regan Williams Prove
Gold Coast City, Queensland, Australia

Terranova Consulting
Gold Coast City, Queensland, Australia

Civil Dimensions
Gold Coast City, Queensland, Australia

Civil Engineer

Morrison Geotech
Gold Coast City, Queensland, Australia

At three-fourths completion, Varsity Lakes already is a successful master-planned community, as defined by market acceptance. When built out, projected for within three to five years, the new community on the shores of Lake Orr in Gold Coast City will have 3,000 residential units, employ 4,500 people, and educate 2,500 students up to grade 12. In short, Varsity Lakes illustrates as much a sustainability strategy as a large-scale real estate development project.

At the southeast corner of Queensland, 60 minutes south of Brisbane, Gold Coast City is Australia's seventh most populous city, known for its recreational opportunities in a subtropical setting. Just 2.5 kilometers (1.6 mi) inland from the ocean is Lake Orr; adjacent to the 343-hectare (848 ac) greenfield parcel are the 2,800-student Bond University, Australia's first private, nonsectarian university, and the 18-hole Robina Woods championship golf course. Here, Delfin Lend Lease, Lend Lease's Australian master-planned community builder, collaborated with the Gold Coast City Council and the state government to establish an economic development strategy (EDS) for job creation and the economic sustainability of the new community.

More than a byword, economic sustainability was planned into Varsity Lakes by the developer's commitment to creating 4,500 full-time jobs on site and by the city's acceptance of home businesses as a permitted use in all residential areas at Varsity Lakes. The EDS established ongoing research and active management to identify the need for such soft programming as a business incubation program and a monthly networking meeting.

Varsity Lakes' master plan is influenced most of all by the community's major amenity, Lake Orr. An extensive system of lakeside linear parks allows public use and provides pedestrian and bicycle connectivity to commercial and mixed-use areas, on and off site. A modified grid system of residential streets encourages passive solar orientation of houses, walkable neighborhoods, and passive surveillance of public areas. The variety of lot sizes increases diversity and varying densities (25 to 50 units per hectare/10 to 20 units per acre) of house forms and types. Between the outlying residential neighborhoods and the mixed-use precinct, transitional housing forms such as lofts are encouraged. Multifamily rental housing is permitted within the mixed-use precinct. This diversity of housing types makes it easy to move up or down the housing scale as residents' space and living requirements change. A revealing statistic is that 30 percent of all home sales are made to existing households.

The mixed-use precinct is synergistically situated next to Bond University and surrounds 3.57-hectare (8.8 ac) Central Park. Market Square is a retail core; Varsity Central is a business core; and Varsity College's junior and senior high school campuses are located here. Additional commercial precincts—two of

Environmental Engineers

Gilbert & Sutherland
Gold Coast City, Queensland, Australia

Mark Rigby & Associates
Gold Coast City, Queensland, Australia

Planit Consulting
Gold Coast City, Queensland, Australia

WBM
Brisbane, Queensland, Australia

Project Data

Web Page

www.varsitylakes.com.au

Site Area

343 hectares (848 ac)

16 percent common open area
(excluding lake)

Facilities

150,000 square meters (53,820 sf)
commercial area

3,000 residential units

Land Uses

residential, commercial, open space,
educational, and recreational

Start/Completion Dates

August 1999–2010

them on the shores of Lake Orr—and a light industrial zone on the eastern outskirts along a highway are being kept offline until further into the project.

To preserve and enhance Varsity Lakes' environmental resources, the developer produced an environmental management plan that influenced the project's master planning. In addition to its recreational potential, Lake Orr was expanded from its natural 55 hectares (136 ac) to 80 hectares (198 ac) in order to increase stormwater retention. An additional 40 hectares (99 ac) of wetland sites are being constructed. In all, 30 parks of varying sizes and the extensive walkways account for 55 hectares (136 ac) of Varsity Lakes' common open space.

To date, over 2,000 residential units, housing 5,000 people, have been completed, with 250 units constantly underway. Varsity College, now enrolling 2,300 K–12 students, opened only two years after the first houses came online. In 2002, Varsity Lakes' third year, Central Park was opened. The retail core, Market Square, was launched in 2004, and the Varsity Central business area now hosts 180 businesses with over 2,500 employees. The expanded Lake Orr now surrounds the newly created Azzurra Island, at 22 hectares (54 ac) large enough to accommodate four parks and 178 lots for single-family detached housing. The lake expansion has added 4.2 kilometers (2.6 mi) of community-use shoreline to Lake Orr and makes it the largest recreational lake in the Gold Coast region. Over AU$270 million (US$203 million) in sales have been recorded throughout Varsity Lakes, and the entire project valuation is extrapolated to exceed AU$1 billion (US$752 million) by buildout in 2010.

CIVIC

ANADOLU HEALTH CENTER

Gebze-Kocaeli, Turkey

Development Team

Owner/Developer

Anadolu Health and Education Foundation
Içerenköy-Istanbul, Turkey
www.anadolusaglik.org

Architect

HAS Mimarlik, Ltd., Rees Architecture Planning Interiors
Zincirlikuyu-Istanbul, Turkey
www.hasmimarlik.com.tr

Landscape Design

DS Mimarlik, Peyzaj Mimarliği, Restorasyon San., Ltd.
Beyoğlu-Istanbul, Turkey
www.trafomimarlar.com

The goal of this state-of-the-art hospital and health care center is to be the best health care provider in Eurasia, offering international-quality care to an area that was devastated by a catastrophic earthquake in 1999. Located 70 kilometers (43.5 mi) southeast of Istanbul, the Anadolu Health Center was developed by the Anadolu Health and Education Foundation on a 20-hectare (49 ac) site provided by the government for a period of 49 years. The health center is an affiliate of the U.S.-based Johns Hopkins Medical Center and has benefited from the contributions of a number of international advisers, ranging from medical equipment specialists to seismic consultants.

The 45,000-square-meter (484,376 sf) center, which includes a 209-bed hospital, incorporates a variety of health-related uses within medical, residential, and educational zones. Encompassing a wide range of health services—from preventive medicine to a rehabilitation center, an oncology center, a nursing home, and a hospice—the center, when completed, also will contain a 240-student nursing school, a 360-student allied health education school, a student dormitory, a 150-room hotel for patients' relatives, and housing for nurses. A green space in the middle of the site connects the center's three zones, and all buildings offer unobstructed sea views. Circulation routes for patients, visitors, and employees have been separated to maximize patient privacy.

Because the center is located in a seismic zone at the epicenter of the 1999 earthquake, extraordinary design precautions were taken to ensure that it will remain fully functional during future earthquakes or other emergencies. All foundations were sunk seven meters (23 feet) below ground level, the ten- by ten-meter (33 by 33 ft) column grid provides an open floor plate, and concrete waffle slabs minimize vibration in operating rooms. The designers, REES Associates, Inc., and HAS Architects Ltd., followed both American Institute of Architects guidelines for hospital and health care facilities and National Fire Protection Association regulations. Nearly 35 percent of the facility's physicians are board certified in the United States.

In addition to providing medical services for patients who come from throughout Turkey, the center also benefits the immediate community by hosting conferences for doctors who work in small towns nearby, providing medical examinations at area schools, and preparing leaflets on healthy living for local newspapers. The foundation's benefactors—a group of companies that contribute a percentage of their profits to the foundation each year—also have donated a primary school for the region.

Project Data

Web Page

www.anadolusaglik.org

Site Area

20 hectares (49 ac)

Facilities

45,000 square meters (484,392 sf) gross
building area
209 hospital rooms
329 surface parking spaces

Land Uses

hospital, educational, parking

Start/Completion Dates

April 2000–February 2005

Planning for the project began in April 2000 but hit a roadblock during Turkey's 2001 economic crisis, when interest rates rose to 7,500 percent overnight and the Turkish lira was devalued by 40 percent. The project was reevaluated after the crisis and value engineering efforts undertaken to ensure that it could be completed. Because every element of the project was planned in minute detail before ground breaking, construction took only two years. Substantially completed in February 2005, the approximately $100 million Anadolu Health Center will break even in 2006—despite caring for 10 percent of its patients without payment—and should achieve a return on investment of 7 percent in 2007 and 13.5 percent in 2008, when it is expected to reach full capacity. At that point, the center will be able to finance new investments with internal funds. In addition to its strong financial performance, the facility has succeeded in reversing Turkey's health care "brain drain," as internationally trained Turkish physicians return to the country to work there.

COLORADO CONVENTION CENTER EXPANSION

Denver, Colorado

Development Team

Owner/Developer

City and County of Denver
Denver, Colorado
www.denvergov.org

Architect

Fentress Bradburn Architects
Denver, Colorado
www.fentressbradburn.com

Associate Architects

Bertram A. Bruton & Associates
Denver, Colorado
www.babassociates.net

Harold Massop Associates
Denver, Colorado
www.hmaarchitects.net

The Abo Group
Denver, Colorado
www.theabogroup.com

Landscape Architect

Civitas, Inc.
Denver, Colorado
www.civitasinc.com

Civil Engineer

The Lund Partnership, Inc.
Lakewood, Colorado

The expansion of the Colorado Convention Center to 2.4 million square feet (222,960 m²) has enabled the facility to host national-scale events, leveraged its location on a light-rail line, and reinforced the identities of both 14th Street, Denver's cultural boulevard, and 16th Street, its pedestrian mall, located just two blocks away. The expanded convention center is an integral part of downtown Denver and a commendable example of responsible urban infill development.

With voter approval, city officials decided in 1999 to more than double the size of the existing convention center, which had opened in 1990. Construction began in January 2001, and the expanded and renovated center opened in December 2004. The project's key design features are its two main facades, which engage both the distant mountain vistas to the west and the vibrant city life to the east. On the western side, a high-peaked, 662-foot-long (202 m) roofline and an 800-foot (244 m) full-facade glass curtain wall are lit at night, creating a new identity for the western perimeter of downtown Denver. On the eastern side, which opens into the heart of downtown, four angular roof blades along another 800-foot (244 m) glass facade facing 14th Street acknowledge the significance and grandeur of this civic facility, while maintaining a friendly and inviting front door from the streetscape.

Inside, a grand concourse known as "the Spine" reinforces the city's urban grid as it connects the building's two sides, intuitively guiding people through 76,000 square feet (70,604 m²) of lobbies and prefunction spaces to the 600,000-square-foot (5,574 m²) exhibit hall, 85,000 square feet (7,897 m²) of ballrooms, and 100,000 square feet (9,290 m²) of meeting rooms, as well as to small breakout rooms and a new 5,000-seat theater that has become one of the city's most popular concert venues. A 25-foot-wide (7.6 m), 110-foot-long (33.5 m) pedestrian bridge connects the convention center with the city's performing arts complex, providing shelter during inclement weather and reducing vehicular and pedestrian congestion. Docks and service areas are well hidden from public view; undulating, perforated stainless steel panels mask 54 truck berths and 1,000 new parking spaces. The design team faced the additional challenge of constructing a contiguous floor plate for the center without compromising a street and light-rail connection that ran through the site. Rather than burying them in a tunnel, designers relocated the street and rail line to the site's northern edge, enabling the relocation and expansion of a light-rail station. An extensive art program commissioned ten artists to create works that have been placed both inside and outside the center.

With its integration of public art and architecture, the expanded Colorado Convention Center strikes a balance between functionality and aesthetics, meeting the needs of conventioneers and the community while adding a striking new image to the Denver skyline. Now capable of handling 95 percent of the nation's convention business, the expanded center generated $145 million more in direct, indirect, and associated spending and an additional $8 million in annual tax revenue in 2005 over the previous year's results, as well as 8,980 new jobs.

"The scope of the expansion of the Colorado Convention Center was momentous, and the steadfast commitment to the project on behalf of the city and county of Denver as the facility owner and developer was vital," comments Jack Finlaw, director of theaters and arenas for the city and county of Denver. "Now that the expansion is complete and the performance of the facility is exceeding our projections, it is clear that the Colorado Convention Center will play an essential role in the success of Denver as a destination city. As a result of the expansion, Denver is benefiting both economically and socially through the creation of jobs, expanded tourism and convention business, and increased revenues."

Project Data

Web Page

www.denverconvention.com

Site Area

30 acres (12 ha)

Facilities

1.4 million square feet (130,064 m²) new gross building area

1 million square feet (92,903 m²) renovated gross building area

1,000 new structured parking spaces

Land Uses

convention/exhibition space, parking

Start/Completion Dates

January 2001–December 2004

HAI RIVER REVITALIZATION

Tianjin, China

Development Team

Owner/Developer

**Haihe Economic Development Office
Tianjin, China**

*Master Planner/
Landscape Architect*

**EDAW, Ltd.
Hong Kong, China**

Project Data

Site Area

4.9 kilometers (3 mi) public riverfront

Facilities

public open space

Start/Completion Dates

**May 2003–September 2004
(Cultural Heritage District)**

The Hai River, part of the great Haihe River system, the largest in northern China, cuts through the center of Tianjin and connects the city to its ocean port 70 kilometers (43 mi) southeast and to Beijing 137 kilometers (85 mi) northwest. In that respect, the Hai is Tianjin's frontyard; but it is its backyard as well, treated as it is with urban waste. The river plays a crucial role in the city's commerce, flood discharge, and water storage and in giving identity to Tianjin's urban environment.

To increase Tianjin's competitiveness in the global marketplace, in 2002 the city formed a team of international consultants, including the Hong Kong office of EDAW, Ltd., to formulate a Hai River development plan that would stimulate overall economic investment by revitalizing the riverfront. The master plan called for improvements along both riverbanks for 20 continuous kilometers (12.4 mi) through the city, to be completed in four stages. The pilot program would be the farthest upriver: the Cultural Heritage District, a 4.9-kilometer (3 mi) stretch that was completed in 2004. The remaining segments have not been fully designed yet. Next downriver is the Urban Entertainment District, 2.2 kilometers (1.4 mi) long, passing through Tianjin's historic shopping and recreation district. The Central Business District, 2.9 kilometers (1.8 mi) long, encompasses the commercial heart of the city. Along this stretch of the river is a rich heritage of colonial architecture—mostly detached villa-style merchant houses—found in the former French, British, and German concessions on the southwest bank. Smart Town District, 10 kilometers (6.2 mi) long, passes through a partially undeveloped portion of the city where Tianjin expects to build an ecological community incorporating high technology.

The development plan states six objectives that unify the master plan and its four phased development districts: Highlight the long and varied history and culture of the city; attract industry to the waterfront area; identify city landmarks by the river; protect the ecological environment of the watershed; improve accessibility to the river; and develop tourism and recreation along the river. Some key elements of public infrastructure that contribute to the revitalization include roads, bridges, water transports, water purification, embankment renovation, lighting, greenery and landscape, environmental arts, and public buildings.

EDAW's master plan accomplishes these objectives with a continuous public waterfront and promenade forming a green spine that provides the structure for the bordering urban land development. The average width of public land fronting the river, defining the edge of the green spine, is 50 meters (164 ft)

on each bank. Riverfront lands are reoriented to the river, integrating new adjacent land uses with the public transportation system.

The Cultural Heritage District was completed in 15 months at a cost of RMB 300 million (US$36 million). Though incomplete, the revitalization has stimulated some significant economic growth and the perception of a more business-friendly environment. Many factories along the river have relocated elsewhere to create room for new commercial and cultural facilities. New investments in riverfront real estate have been responsible for the redevelopment of 30,000 housing units in adjacent residential neighborhoods, generating demand for 2 million square meters (21.5 million sf) of new residential space and achieving RMB 6 million (US$720,000) in transaction volume. Since 2000, two years before planning began, land prices along the Hai River has been increasing at an annualized rate of 30 percent. Tourism has also increased, encouraging the central shopping district to expand its area from 20,000 square meters (215,278 sf) to 200,000 square meters (2.15 million sf).

LOS ANGELES UNIFIED SCHOOL DISTRICT CONSTRUCTION PROGRAM

Los Angeles, California

For nearly three decades, the Los Angeles Unified School District (LAUSD) had no comprehensive construction program and had not built a single new high school. The nation's second largest school district—which spans more than 704 square miles (1,824 km²) and serves 727,000 students living in Los Angeles and 26 additional municipalities—was in the throes of an overcrowding crisis, forced to bus thousands of students to schools many miles outside their communities and to place more than half of the district's student population on an abbreviated academic calendar. Moreover, the city and surrounding municipalities were running out of land on which new, large-scale schools could be built.

To resolve this crisis, the LAUSD Facilities Services Division is now engaged in the largest new-school construction program in U.S. history. The result of several voter-approved state and local bond measures, this ambitious, $11.7 billion new-school construction program is well on its way toward delivering state-of-the-art new neighborhood schools—including primary centers, elementary schools, middle schools, high schools, and continuation high schools—as well as expanding existing schools. The program aims to help every school becoming a center of its community, creating not only a sense of neighborhood pride but also, in partnership with other public and private entities, providing the green space, gathering places, and recreational facilities that are sorely needed throughout greater Los Angeles. "We're building more than 150 new schools for the students of Los Angeles, and when our new construction program is complete in 2012, we will have built the equivalent of San Diego's entire school district right here in Los Angeles," notes Jim McConnell, chief facilities executive for the LAUSD. "There has not been a more important construction program in Los Angeles since William Mulholland brought the Owens River to this city."

Traditional school planning guides typically recommend (and, in some states, require) minimum site sizes for schools, generally from 14 acres (6 ha) for a 400-student elementary school up to 50 acres (20 ha) for a 2,000-student high school. But such large land parcels simply are not available (or affordable) today in greater Los Angeles. The LAUSD therefore has skillfully adapted these criteria to the region's

Development Team

Owner/Developer

**Los Angeles Unified School District
Los Angeles, California
www.lausd.net**

Architects

(this partial list only includes architects for the schools depicted here)

**Arquitectonica
Los Angeles, California
www.arquitectonica.com**

**Gensler
Santa Monica, California
www.gensler.com**

**Gonzalez/Goodale Architects
Pasadena, California
www.gonzalezgoodale.com**

**Leidenfrost/Horowitz &
Associates, Inc.
Glendale, California
www.lhaarchitects.com**

**Nadel Architects, Inc.
Los Angeles, California
www.nadelarc.com**

dense urban landscape with solutions that include vertical construction, placing parking underground (and reducing parking requirements), building shared facilities, partnering with other public and private entities, combining traditional and continuation high schools, and expanding facilities on existing school campuses. With these methods, the district is demonstrating that innovative design and the resourceful use of available land make the standard 50-acre high school site (which could potentially displace more than 60 housing units) unnecessary. Through innovative public/private partnerships, the LAUSD is building new schools that meet particular community needs and provide valuable new resources.

By the end of 2005, the LAUSD new-school construction program had delivered 55 new schools and 37 additions to existing schools, 19 early education centers, and 14 playground expansions. These efforts have provided 1,826 new classrooms and new seats for 46,180 students to date. The new schools encompass more than 3.6 million square feet (334,440 m²) and occupy more than 240 acres (97 ha) of land. They include pioneering facilities such as Orthopaedic High School, which shares facilities with the neighboring Orthopaedic Hospital; Dr. Theodore T. Alexander Jr. Science Center School, the result of a collaboration with the California Science Center; and Canoga Park Elementary School, a charter school that is part of an innovative master-planned, mixed-income community. The LAUSD is changing the face of Los Angeles, building community focal points that will provide the city's children with the best possible education in schools built for the children of today and generations to come.

PBWS Architects
Pasadena, California
www.pbws.com

Rachlin Architects
Culver City, California
www.rachlinarchitects.com

R.L. Binder, FAIA Architecture and Planning
Playa del Rey, California
www.binderarchitects.com

tBP/Architecture
Los Angeles, California
www.tbparch.com

Westberg + White, Inc.
Tustin, California
www.wwarch.com

William Loyd Jones Architect
Venice, California

Project Data

Web Page

www.laschools.org

Facilities

new: 55 completed/150 planned
additions: 37 completed/80 planned
seats: 50,000 completed/170,000 planned

Land Uses

educational, civic, public recreational

Start/Completion Dates

2001–2012

Jury Statement

In 2001, after almost 30 years of inattention, the country's second largest public school district launched a $19 billion, 230-facility construction and expansion program in a city with little space for traditional school development. The program is being innovatively and cost effectively planned and implemented on a fast track, in support of the school district's mission of educating children "to their maximum potential."

LUOHU LAND PORT AND TRAIN STATION

Shenzhen, China

The border crossing at Luohu, connecting Shenzhen on the mainland with Hong Kong, is China's busiest, with 400,000 people passing through each day (and as many as 600,000 on holidays). Because travelers between the mainland and Hong Kong must pass through customs, the checkpoint—where mainland rail, subway, and bus lines converge—has always been a bottleneck for both pedestrians and multimodal traffic. Now, with the completion of the Luohu Land Port and Train Station, the three-city-block area is a ceremonial gateway to China and a public amenity for the citizens of Shenzhen and its many visitors.

As one of 14 special economic zones (SEZ) in China, the 7.5-kilometer-wide (4.7 mi) area along the Shenzhen border enjoys expanded free trade and enterprise opportunities geared toward foreign markets. The Shenzhen SEZ, established in 1979, was singled out as the first in China because of its proximity to Hong Kong. It was thought that here capitalism had the best chance of taking root in communist China.

With the institution of a free-market economy in the SEZ, prices for consumer goods became cheaper here than in Hong Kong, attracting many residents and tourists from Hong Kong, long before Hong Kong became a special administrative region (SAR) of China in 1997. The greatly increased economic activity accelerated the SEZ area's need for infrastructure construction, including passenger and freight rail and long- and short-haul buses. In December 2004, a 23.75-kilometer (14.75 mi) subway was opened from Luohu to Shenzhen airport west of the city (the completion date was coordinated with the completion of Luohu Land Port). In combination with the traditional taxis, private vehicles, and the busy pedestrian traffic of the commercial core of Shenzhen—coming and going to work and shopping—the customs checkpoint became a maelstrom of conflicting activity.

Planning in concert with the private businesses that stood to prosper from a newly revitalized inter-modal transport facility, the city's land administration agency committed RMB 700 million (US$87.5 million) to build a new, multilevel land port (and an additional RMB 200 million/US$25 million for infra-structure improvements). Private money paid for the train stations and refurbishment of the surrounding retail, hotel, and restaurant facilities. At the upper level is a 400-meter-long (1,312 ft) open-air plaza with bamboo gardens on both sides. A continuous trellis of bougainvillea provides shade and unifies, at the pedestrian level, the various architectural styles that surround the plaza. Openings in the plaza for stairs, escalators, and sunken gardens bring light to the lower levels. At the lower levels, rail, bus, subway, and vehicular traffic are sorted out with terminals, pedestrianways, and clear signage.

Development Team

Owner/Developer

Shenzhen Municipal Planning Bureau
Shenzhen, China

Urban Designer

SWA Group
Houston, Texas
www.swagroup.com

Master Planner

Chinese Academy of Planning and
Urban Design
Shenzhen, China

Site Designer

Shenzhen Municipal Engineering
Design Institute
Shenzhen, China

Transportation Designer

Beijing Urban Engineering Design &
Research Institute Company, Ltd.
Shenzhen, China
www.buedri.com

Design Consultant

Shenzhen BLY Landscape &
Architecture, Planning & Urban
Design Institute
Shenzhen, China

Project Data

Site Area

37.5 hectares (92.7 ac)

Parking Facilities

6,000 surface parking spaces

8,200 structured parking spaces

Land Uses

public open space, transportation,
retail, parking

Start/Completion Dates

December 2001–December 2004

Jury Statement

This border control and multiple transportation center at China's busiest
gateway, the Hong Kong–Shenzhen
border, was transformed into an
efficient and user-friendly intermodal
transportation hub and multilevel
public space serving the needs of the
400,000 people who pass through
each day.

MESA ARTS CENTER

Mesa, Arizona

Development Team

Owner/Developer

Mesa Arts Center
Mesa, Arizona
www.mesaartscenter.com

Design Architect

BOORA Architects, Inc.
Portland, Oregon
www.boora.com

Architect of Record

DWL Architects + Planners, Inc.
Phoenix, Arizona
www.dwlarchitects.com

Landscape Architect

Martha Schwartz, Inc.
Cambridge, Massachusetts
www.marthaschwartz.com

Landscape Architect of Record

Design Workshop
Tempe, Arizona
www.designworkshop.com

The Mesa Arts Center is a promising first step toward establishing an urban center for Arizona's third largest city, a sprawling outgrowth of Phoenix with no nucleus or recognizable visual identity. "As Mesa has grown over the past three decades, so has its cultural fabric," notes Gerry Fathauer, the center's executive director. "Extensive workshops, classes, productions, and performances have become a constant. In 1998, a voter-approved quality-of-life sales tax propelled the building of the Mesa Arts Center in the heart of downtown, elevating the local arts and attracting international touring artists. The new Mesa Arts Center, a 212,750-square-foot (19,765 m²) visual and performing arts complex, celebrates a convergence of the environment, the arts, and the community of Mesa, forging dialogue between artists and audiences for generations, and seasons, to come."

Set on a seven-acre (three ha) campus directly across from city hall, the public arts complex contains galleries and other exhibit spaces, four theaters, studios, classrooms, and administrative offices, as well as a large outdoor plaza and passageway. The project celebrates the essence of the Southwest while offering

Project Data

Web Page

www.mesaartscenter.com

Site Area

7 acres (2.8 ha)

36 percent open space

Facilities

212,755 square feet (19,765 m²)
gross building area

150 surface parking spaces

330 structured parking spaces

Land Uses

cultural, public open spaces, parking

Start/Completion Dates

1998–2004

Jury Statement

The Mesa Arts Center establishes a cultural arts anchor in downtown Mesa, a sprawling outgrowth of Phoenix, which before had had no nucleus. It brings to the city of Mesa a new performing arts venue, a museum, a major art school, and outdoor civic spaces, providing a stimulating urban center with all of the cultural, social, and economic benefits.

comprehensive performance and visual arts programming and education and creating an economic development engine for downtown Mesa.

The design team aimed to reflect the extreme qualities of the desert landscape: the hot, dry climate, the desire for shade, and the intense character of the sunlight. The design scheme is an urban "geode," a central framework of buildings with a solid exterior containing a sparkling interior gem. This structure provides a street wall for a city that lacked density and needed spatial definition. The result is a block of development with three buildings featuring jagged angles, canted and glass walls, sloping roofs, and regional colors and materials. This block was then "cracked" open to create an elaborate passageway with a civic space that functions as a pedestrian street and entry spaces for the theaters. This passageway evolved into the Shadow Walk, a grand promenade that intersects the complex in a bold, arching gesture, providing small parks and water features as well as opportunities for gatherings, performances, and outdoor exhibits. Plantings are displayed in ways that dramatize their shadow patterns, while also creating comfortable spaces for visitors. Paralleling the Shadow Walk is the Arroyo, a water feature with a southwestern narrative.

Public funding of $94.5 million from the city's quality-of-life sales tax was supplemented by $3.7 million from the Mesa Arts Alliance, a nonprofit group, for a total capital budget of $90.8 million. Before the center opened, another nonprofit partner, the Mesa Arts Center Foundation, pledged to raise hundreds of thousands of dollars in operating funds and to establish an endowment fund to bolster the center's financial stability.

Ground breaking took place in May 2002, and the Mesa Arts Center opened to the public in spring 2005. Halfway through its first year of operation, the center was operating on budget; 350,000 to 500,000 people are expected to visit each year, attending the center's 600 to 800 annual performances and participating in year-round classes and exhibits. The center has stimulated interest in downtown redevelopment, and new restaurants, businesses, and a condominium project are in the works. The Mesa Arts Center offers a shining example of the power of collaboration among a community, a design team, and forward-thinking civic leaders, demonstrating how an arts center can be the spark that lights the flame of smart urban redevelopment.

MUZIEKGEBOUW AAN 'T IJ

Amsterdam, The Netherlands

Amsterdam's city council had long dreamed of bringing the city center back to the waterfront of the IJ, a broad river dividing the city into two parts. Although the original city center had been located along the southern bank of the IJ, development in the early 20th century separated the city's urban core from the water and, until recently, this area was an active harbor inaccessible to the public. After years of planning that began in the 1980s, the city is now redeveloping a long strip of land on the south side of the IJ with an urban master plan that calls for a mix of housing, offices, public buildings, and other civic-related functions. The Muziekgebouw aan 't IJ (Music Hall on the IJ) is playing a fundamental role in this revitalization effort.

Owned and developed by the city's ministry of cultural affairs and completely financed by the city council, the Muziekgebouw aan 't IJ is a 15,850-square-meter (170,607 sf) structure containing three performance halls: a multifunction main auditorium that seats 800 to 1,000; a smaller, 100-seat concert hall; and the BIMhuis, a concert hall designed for jazz and improvisational performances that seats 350 to 400. The building also features rehearsal spaces and offices that the city leases to a variety of orchestras, foundations, and other music-related organizations. An enormous flat roof accentuates the structure's location at the beginning of a long strip of new development. Cleverly designed as a concrete box surrounded by a transparent glass shell, the facility incorporates cutting-edge acoustic technology, providing optimal sound transmission on a minimal budget while making a dramatic statement along the waterfront and offering breathtaking views of the water and the city.

The structure's concrete walls were cast in place to maximize sound isolation. Movable floors and ceilings within the concert halls can adjust the volume of the space as well as acoustic resonance. Three primary colors—natural concrete, black, and the light maple wood used in the floors and the main auditorium paneling—tie together the building's various elements. The glass shell has been built in a rough industrial style that exposes its structural elements and reflects the waterfront's industrial history while accommodating all the center's public spaces and offices.

By developing this facility, the city has made an excellent start in returning the waterfront to the community. Since it was completed in fall 2004 and opened in summer 2005, the Muziekgebouw has become a popular gathering spot and an architectural showplace. By making a conscious choice to develop a noncommercial facility in this pivotal location, the city council has succeeded in attracting commercial investors to the surrounding area. As residential and commercial development continue, the structure's role in the revitalization process that is converting this once industrial zone into a civic space will become even more apparent.

Development Team

Owner/Developer

Dienst Maatschappelijke Ontwikkeling (City of Amsterdam Department of Cultural Affairs) Amsterdam, The Netherlands www.dmo.amsterdam.nl

Architect

3XN Århus, Denmark www.3xn.dk

Project Manager

ABT bv Arnhem, Amsterdam, The Netherlands www.abt-consult.nl

Project Data

Web Page
www.muziekgebouw.nl

Site Area
1.5 hectares (3.7 ac)

Facilities
15,850 square meters (170,607 sf) gross building area

550 surface parking spaces

Land Uses
cultural, parking

Start/Completion Dates
Spring 2002–Summer 2005

Jury Statement

The Muziekgebouw introduces a new, cultural use to the ongoing development of the IJ riverfront, which until recently was an active harbor and inaccessible to the public. This 1,000-seat concert hall—and associated, smaller venues within a 15,850-square-meter (170,608 sf) building—supports the residential and commercial development that is transforming the IJ River from an industrial zone to a vibrant civic amenity.

NEW MILAN
FAIR COMPLEX

Milan, Italy

Development Team

Owner/Developer

Fondazione Fiera Milano
Milan, Italy
www.fondazionefieramilano.com

Architect

Massimiliano Fuksas architetto
Rome, Italy
www.fuksas.it

Associate Architects

Schlaich Bergermann und Partner
Stuttgart, Germany
www.sbp.de

Studio Altieri
Thiene (VI), Italy
www.studioaltieri.it

Studio Marzullo
Rome, Italy

Parking Structure Architect

Mario Bellini Associati
Milan, Italy
www.bellini.it

Hotel Architect

DPA Dominique Perrault Architecture
Paris, France
www.perraultarchitecte.com

The New Milan Fair Complex (Nuovo Sistema Fiera Milano) has transformed a brownfield site along the main road from downtown Milan to Malpensa Airport into a 200-hectare (494 ac) exhibition center, relieving traffic congestion around the historic fairground in the city center and allowing the original fairground to continue to host smaller congresses and trade shows, even after part of the downtown site is sold and redeveloped. The two separate yet complementary developments—the new complex at Rho-Pero (popularly known as Fieramilano) and the downtown complex (known as Fieramilanocity)—have brought new life and prestige to Milan's exhibition industry, enabling the Milan Fair Complex to continue competing with other European exhibition centers and to maintain its position as an international leader. Both projects are being promoted by Fondazione Fiera Milano, the private company that owns and operates the Milan Fair Complex, through its subsidiary Sviluppo Sistema Fiera SpA.

The site of the new complex at Rho-Pero, two adjoining industrial suburbs northwest of Milan, was long occupied by an Agip oil refinery. After Fondazione Fiera Milano purchased the site, the refinery was dismantled and the land and groundwater cleaned up. In an approach considered highly unusual and innovative in Italy, the foundation issued an international request for proposals (RFP) to select a general contractor, an approach that lent continuity and consistency to the design and construction stages and resulted in more accurate cost estimates and quicker completion. Construction of the new complex began in October 2002 and was completed just 30 months later on March 31, 2005. The complex consists of eight multipurpose pavilions built along a 1.3-kilometer-long (4,265 ft) central avenue covered by a futuristic glass-and-steel structure undulating to a height of 36 meters (118 ft) above the Service and Congress Center. The complex covers more than 2 million square meters (21.5 million sf) and has a footprint of 530,000 square meters (5.7 million sf).

Although the €750 million cost of the new complex was funded entirely by Fondazione Fiera Milano, the cooperation of all parties involved was essential to the project's success. Fondazione Fiera Milano collaborated with a wide range of public authorities and organizations, including the Regional Council of Lombardy, the Provincial Council of Milan, the City Council of Milan, the suburban councils of Rho and Pero, and other local groups to ensure that the new and redeveloped complexes would benefit all. "Fondazione Fiera Milano established—right from the outset—a method wholly new for Italy, one based on alliances among everyone involved in the operation: institutions, businesses, and government, as well

Project Data

Web Page

www.nuovosistemafieramilano.it

Site Area

200 hectares (494 ac)
9 percent public green space

Facilities

590,000 square meters (6,350,707 sf)
gross building area

20,000 surface parking spaces

Land Uses

convention center, parking

Start/Completion Dates

October 2002–March 2005

Jury Statement

The New Milan Fair Complex transforms a brownfield site between Malpensa Airport and downtown Milan into a 200-hectare (494 ac) modern exhibition grounds, relieving Milan's historic fairgrounds, located in the center city, from traffic congestion and enabling it once again to host smaller-scale fairs. Together, the new Milan Fair Complex and the historic fairgrounds have expanded the city's exhibition capacity and strengthened Milan's global competitiveness for large-scale exhibitions.

as on shared goals and liabilities," notes Luigi Roth, chairman and CEO of Fondazione Fiera Milano. Public authorities invested an additional €800 million in transportation infrastructure and connections to the complex. The area's road and highway network is being upgraded to provide better access and connections between the Rho-Pero area, Milan, Malpensa Airport, and the rest of Italy. Milan's subway line is being extended to the site, and a railroad connection is expected to be completed in December 2006.

In a separate 2004 RFP, Fondazione Fiera Milano selected the CityLife consortium to redevelop 255,000 square meters (2.7 million sf) of the 400,000-square-meter (4.3 million sf) historic fairground site in the center of Milan. The transformation of the original Milan Fair Complex into a dual-hub exhibition system is one of the most important forces driving economic growth in northern Italy today. The entire complex is expected to generate €4.3 billion in revenue and to create 42,700 new jobs; it already has made the region a key player in global competition.

SINGAPORE CONSERVATION PROGRAMME

Singapore

By the time the marketing term "competitive advantage" came to be applied to urban design and development, Singapore—a progressive modernist city-state and Southeast Asia's model free-market economy—already was ahead of the world. Singapore not only had a strategically inclined urban development structure, it had in place a program to protect, refurbish, and reuse its cultural heritage. If an ability to manage its complex urban infrastructure gives a city a competitive advantage, Singapore has as much as any.

Singapore's Urban Redevelopment Authority (URA) is a powerful government agency that administers the nation's land use planning function. As an island nation of 4.4 million people on 699 square kilometers (270 mi²)—much of it undevelopable—Singapore is considered to be the third densest country in the world. The URA is charged with wresting the most efficient use of land in a country of 400 public parks. It is a city that is able to call itself the "Garden City" and at the same time catapult itself headlong into ever-increasing density.

After Singapore was established as a British trading post in 1819 by Thomas Stamford Raffles of the British East India Company, foreign trading partners moved into permanent settlements around its central core. Ethnic neighborhoods thus sprang up, such as Chinatown, Little India, and the old Malay neighborhood Kampong Glam. By the 1960s, many of these neighborhoods had deteriorated into slums, due to rapid population growth. Singapore gained its independence from Malaysia in 1965, with Lee Kuan Yew, Singapore's first—and, until 1990, only—prime minister, heading a government that fostered a free-market economy under a strict, corruption-free administration. The government embarked on urban renewal efforts with an emphasis on clearance of slums, public housing (90 percent of the population now lives in government-built housing), and public infrastructure. Its primary goal was the transformation of the city into a modern, efficient center for business and industry.

The slum-clearance policy came into question in 1981, when the URA realized that harbor reclamation projects not only gained enough land for Singapore, they created land where it was most valuable. And in 1983, when tourism dropped 3.5 percent—attributed in part to a perceived lack of native color in a modernizing country—the primary motive for slum clearance disappeared. A new goal emerged: preserve old buildings and neighborhoods to restore tourism, but respect the needs and rights of owners.

This Singapore did, with the same dedication that it had modernized the city. The URA's Conservation Master Plan (1989) established a legal framework for conserving buildings, inviting private development,

Development Team

Sponsor

Urban Redevelopment Authority Singapore www.ura.gov.sg

Project Data

Site Area

699 square kilometers (270 mi²)

Start/Completion Dates

1980s–ongoing

Jury Statement

In a rapidly modernizing country, Singapore has established a model conservation program to preserve its rich heritage of vernacular buildings and colorful neighborhoods. Using a collaborative approach involving government organizations, the public, and developers, the island republic's Urban Redevelopment Authority has achieved a balance between free-market economics and cultural conservation.

encouraging good restoration practices, consulting with the private sector, and promoting conservation through education and recognition. Since then, 6,563 buildings have been designated for conservation. Although no direct subsidies are given to the owners, incentives such as waiver of permitting fees, car parking requirements, and some setback requirements are offered.

There are four levels of conservation, determined by type and location. In the Historic Districts of Chinatown, Little India, Kampong Glam, and Boat Quay, shophouses (attached buildings with shops at street level and residential quarters for the owners above) line many contiguous urban street blocks; their exteriors must be fully preserved, but the interiors may be modernized. Says Koh-Lim Wen Gin, chief planner at the URA, "We don't want to make the guidelines so strict that the owners can't use the houses." In the Residential Historic Districts of Emerald Hill and Cairnhill, located close in on narrow streets, owners are allowed to adapt the interiors to modern standards and to build rear additions no higher than the main roofs of the original houses. In Secondary Settlements such as Joo Chiat and Geylang, developed in the early 1900s at the fringe of the city, where old buildings are surrounded by more recent developments, owners are not expected to surrender economic potential but are guided to build additions that complement the conserved buildings. Finally, the Bungalows, larger detached houses built in a variety of architectural styles in various places away from the city center, are allowed to be added to as long as an addition does not reduce the prominence of the conserved building. If a house occupies a sufficiently large lot, the land may be subdivided.

Singapore's Conservation Programme clearly demonstrates that heritage conservation and modernity are not necessarily in opposition. Its balanced, market-oriented approach encourages owners and developers to restore their properties to accommodate new functions. It thus ensures that old buildings remain economically viable and are well maintained to prolong their life spans.

WASHINGTON CONVENTION CENTER

Washington, D.C.

Despite its six-block-long footprint, the new Washington Convention Center (WCC) does not overwhelm its neighborhood. The supersized, 2.3 million-square-foot (213,670 m²) building—the largest in the city— is well integrated into the historic urban fabric of its surroundings; its inviting, transparent design relates to the streets of Washington, D.C., respecting Pierre L'Enfant's 1791 plan for the city and the low-rise scale of the adjacent neighborhoods.

Washington's previous convention center was the nation's third largest when it opened in 1983, but the national convention and meeting business soon outgrew the facility. The structure—which was dark and gloomy inside and presented blank concrete walls to the street—was unable to attract high-end, smaller gatherings. A lack of room for expansion convinced city officials to build a new center that, while much larger than the original, would avoid its bleak, antiurban image. To fund the $834 million complex, the city taxed hotels and restaurants to secure $507 million worth of bonds; additional financing came from federal and local grants, contracts with vendors, and interest earnings.

Meeting the functional requirements necessary for such a huge building while ensuring that it blended into the city and the neighborhood was quite a challenge. The eventual design solution preserved the street grid with a structure that appeared to be three smaller, connected buildings; this strategy resulted in a center with a more human scale and enabled three important east/west streets to run through it, maintaining the continuity of the street system. To comply with the city's famously strict height limits, the architects buried 40 percent of the center below grade, thus making the most of a tight, 17.1-acre (6.9 ha) site.

In contrast to most convention centers, which house all their exhibit space on one enormous floor, the WCC incorporates an unusual stacked arrangement of exhibit halls and meeting spaces that permits several exhibits and shows to be held simultaneously. Lower levels are flooded with daylight, so that many visitors do not realize they are underground. Washington, D.C., attracts a different kind of convention: mostly of professionals with a reason to be in the nation's capital. These are not megaconventions; they are smaller and require more upscale facilities.

The building's mammoth size also presented significant construction challenges. The decision to place so much of the structure underground required digging a huge hole. Billed as the largest excavation for any new building in the Western Hemisphere, it involved the removal of more than 2 million

Development Team

Owner/Developer

Washington Convention Center Authority
Washington, D.C.

Architect

Thompson, Ventulett, Stainback & Associates
Atlanta, Georgia
www.tvsa.com

Associated Architects

Devrouax & Purnell Architects
Washington, D.C.
www.dp-architects.com

Mariani Architects & Engineers
Washington, D.C.

Landscape Architect

Lee & Liu Associates, Inc.
Washington, D.C.

Project Data

Web Page

www.dcconvention.com

Site Area

14.6 acres (5.9 ha)

Facilities

2.3 million square feet (213,670 m²)
gross building area

150 structured parking spaces

Land Use

convention center

Start/Completion Dates

1998–2003

Jury Statement

The Washington Convention Center—
despite a six-block footprint—manages
not to overwhelm its urban neighborhood, while remaining functional
and contextual in a city of neoclassic
civic buildings and monuments.
Though much of the complex's interior
area is underground, it is daylighted;
and exhibit halls are on multiple levels,
allowing for simultaneous events
targeted to the convention center's
market niche of smaller, high-end
professional meetings.

tons (1.8 million metric tons) of dirt. On the site's perimeter, a 3.5-foot-thick (1.1 m) reinforced concrete slurry wall acts as an inverted bathtub, extending as deep as 75 feet (23 m) in some areas and braced by compression steel struts to hold back earth and water. The building required so much steel that structural elements were fabricated in seven places, including China, Russia, and South Korea. Despite numerous setbacks, the center opened on schedule in mid-2003.

The center's location in the heart of the nation's capital called for an elegant, eye-catching design not generally associated with convention centers. "Distinctive elements incorporated into the building design," notes Michael M. Dickens, chair of the Washington Convention Center Authority's board of directors, "include the dramatic 300-foot (91 m) curved glass entry, skylights, carpet specially designed in and imported from Ireland, and a $4 million art program, which is the largest of any U.S. convention center.

"Approvals were received from the National Capital Planning Commission, the Commission of Fine Arts, and the Historic Preservation Review Board," Dickens continues. "The building's innovative architecture meets all of the functional requirements of a convention center while offering an inviting, light-filled design that respects the low-rise scale of adjacent neighborhoods. The center has sparked a wave of economic development in the adjacent Mount Vernon and Shaw neighborhoods, including new residential development, restaurants, and cultural facilities."

WUXI LI LAKE PARKLANDS

Wuxi, China

In an impressively short time of three years, the city of Wuxi has transformed a neglected lake in a tourism-dependent region into an environmental and civic asset, attracting development investment and expanding the region's tourism base. Li Lake (or Lihu), 5.5 kilometers (3.4 mi) from Wuxi city's center, was run-down, and the shore was crowded with outmoded fish farms, with no space for the public realm. The lake and the waterfront were underused as a public and recreational resource. For a region whose tourism industry accounts for 10 percent of revenue, it was an intolerable situation. Today, in place of the fish farms are an improved shoreline and new parklands of open lawn areas, floral gardens, waterfront promenades and plazas, and attractions for the citizens of Wuxi and visitors.

Li Lake, an offshoot of Tai Lake (Taihu), is part of the largest natural lake environment in China. Long, narrow, and doglegged, Li Lake (9.5 square kilometers/3.7 mi²) is a tourist destination with a number of nationally known sites, and it opens to Tai Lake, the third largest lake in China at 2,250 square kilometers (869 mi²). Only 130 kilometers (81 mi) northwest of Shanghai, Wuxi is undergoing commercial and industrial development that is surpassing its tourism industry.

More than a design solution alone, Wuxi Li Lake Parklands provides an example of increasing land values by enhancing the environment. Wuxi city is leveraging the parklands as an urban asset with New Lake City, a 20-square-kilometer (7.7 mi²) area between the old city and Li Lake. In addition to the Li Lake parklands, New Lake City will have residential neighborhoods, commercial and administrative zones, and educational, recreational, entertainment, and other open-space amenities. Land values in this planned growth area have increased from RMB16,942 to 33,883 per hectare (US$823 to 1,645 per ac) before construction to RMB169,375 (US$8,229 per ac) after construction. The number of visitors has grown 22 percent, and employment has expanded by more than 20,000 in the year since completion of the parklands.

The parklands were completed in three years. Starting from the northwest corner of the lake, where most of the aquacultural farms were located, to an existing causeway across Li Lake, four kilometers (2.5 mi) of shoreline have been restored in two stages with new beachfronts, promenades, boulevards, plazas, shelters, and public art. The first stage included the creation of a small, seven-hectare (17 ac) island, Fishing Dragon Island, and a waterfront plaza, Flame Plaza. The latter will form a connection to the lake from a new, 20-hectare (49 ac) park at the center of New Lake City. The latest waterfront park to be completed is the 24-hectare (59 ac) Bridge Park, which will anchor a planned causeway across the lake to its southern shore. Future projects include a 60-hectare (148 ac) environmental park on the southern shore, which will mark the entrance to the lake of a ten-kilometer (6.2 mi) wetlands corridor to manage stormwater entering the lake.

Development Team

Owner/Developer

Wuxi Lake District Planning & Construction Leading Team Office Wuxi, China

Landscape Architect

EDAW (Shanghai) Shanghai, China www.edaw.com.hk

Architect

Szczepan Urbanowicz Kenmore Hills, Queensland, Australia

Project Data

Site Area

165 hectares (408 ac)

Land Use

public open space

Start/Completion Dates

2002–2005

Jury Statement

As the city of Wuxi expands in the direction of Li Lake, it has begun to restore, protect, and improve the lake and the lands surrounding it, part of China's largest lake environment. Encompassing 165 hectares (408 ac) and 60 percent completed, the project already has enhanced the natural environment in the area, attracted development investment, and provided a human-scale place for people to gather and celebrate

ABOUT THE JURIES

The Americas Jury

Isaac M. Manning, Jury Chair
Fort Worth, Texas

Isaac Manning is president of Trinity Works, a real estate company he founded in 2002. During his more than 20 years of experience as an architect and developer, Manning has focused on public/private partnerships that have become economic development success stories, and he has acquired a global network of cross-disciplinary relationships. Trinity Works has provided development expertise on public and private sector projects in Texas, North Carolina, Missouri, and Arizona, and is developing a number of small and large mixed-use projects in Texas and South Carolina.

Manning spent 13 years at Hillwood Development Corporation and worked as an architect for Swanke Hayden Connell Architects and CHK Architects (now Torri Gallas and Partners), both Washington, D.C.–based firms. He holds an undergraduate degree from Vanderbilt University and graduate degrees from Virginia Polytechnic Institute and State University and the Massachusetts Institute of Technology. He is a member of the American Institute of Architects and the Urban Land Institute (ULI).

Lee T. Hanley, Vice Chair
Phoenix, Arizona

Lee Hanley is a founding principal of Phoenix-based Vestar Development Company and has been its CEO since 1989. He is currently responsible for strategic planning, capital market affiliations, and executive oversight of Vestar Development Company and Vestar Property Management.

Previously, Hanley held positions at Estes Development Company, CB Commercial, and Xerox Corporation. He is a graduate of the University of Arizona with a degree in accounting, and he has served as an officer in the U.S. Marine Corps, including duty in Vietnam.

Lee is a trustee of ULI; serves on the boards of the Phi Gamma Delta Educational Foundation, Greater Phoenix Leadership, International Council of Shopping Centers, Lambda Alpha International, Valley Partnership, Center for Design Excellence at Arizona State University, and Valley of the Sun United Way; and is active in several other civic and cultural organizations in the Phoenix area.

Ronald A. Altoon
Los Angeles, California

Ronald Altoon is a partner of Altoon + Porter Architects, LLP, an international architectural, urban design, and planning firm with professional practice entities in Los Angeles, Amsterdam, Hong Kong, and Moscow. He is responsible for designs for complex projects in Asia, Australia, the Middle East, Europe, and the United States.

Altoon's practice encompasses urban infill, commercial mixed-use, higher education, transit, and residential projects. He has authored three books on the work of his firm, as well as one for the retail industry on international projects.

A ULI leader, Altoon served on the ULI New York World Trade Center Summit 2006 Blue Ribbon Panel and speaks at ULI conferences, both domestic and international. He was national president in 1998 of the American Institute of Architects. He holds a bachelor's degree in architecture from the University of Southern California and a master's degree in architecture from the University of Pennsylvania.

Barbara Faga
Atlanta, Georgia

Barbara Faga is chair of the board of EDAW, Inc., global environmental, economic, planning, and design consultants. She has directed complex teams on large, time-sensitive, and award-winning projects that include preservation plans, retail projects, downtown revitalization plans, waterfront development, parks and recreation projects, land management plans, and housing and community development projects. She has worked for the cities of Atlanta, Georgia, and Alexandria, Virginia, as a landscape architect and urban designer and is the author of *Designing Public Consensus* (Wiley, 2006).

Educated at the Georgia Institute of Technology and Michigan State University, Faga has held numerous academic appointments and received a number of professional honors and awards. Her professional affiliations include member of the executive committee of the American Society of Landscape Architects; chair of the Landscape Architecture Foundation; cochair of the Green Ribbon Committee for Atlanta Parks, Open Space, and Greenways Plan; and chair of the Atlanta Urban Design Commission. She currently serves on ULI's Program Committee.

Richard F. Galehouse
Watertown, Massachusetts

Richard Galehouse is a principal and senior planner at Sasaki Associates, Inc., a multidisciplinary professional services firm with an international practice in planning, architecture, landscape architecture, civil engineering, interior design, and graphic design. He has been with Sasaki since 1961 and has served as principal-in-charge of planning and urban design and as principal of the firm's various governing boards.

Galehouse's professional practice areas encompass mixed-use real estate development; urban planning; and new community, resort, institutional, regional, and environmental planning and design. He is a frequent contributor to *Urban Land* magazine.

A longtime ULI member, Galehouse has served on many councils, plan analysis panels, and Advisory Services panels. He is affiliated with the American Institute of Architects, the American Institute of Certified Planners, and Lambda Alpha International. Galehouse received a bachelor's degree in architecture from the University of Notre Dame and a master's of city and regional planning degree from Harvard University's Graduate School of Design.

Timur Fisk Galen
New York, New York

Timur Galen is global head of corporate services and real estate at Goldman Sachs & Company.

Prior to joining Goldman Sachs in 2002, Galen worked as an executive with the Walt Disney Corporation and Reichmann International, LP. He is a registered architect, having completed his design apprenticeship with Pritzker Prize–winning architects Robert Venturi (Venturi, Scott Brown and Associates) and Fumihiko Maki.

Galen is a trustee of MASS MoCA, a director of the Forum for Urban Design and the Alliance for Downtown New York, a member of ULI, and serves on the boards of the Steven Newman Real Estate Institute, Baruch College/The City University of New York, and the Property Committee of Inwood House. He is also past chair of the Haverford College Annual Fund and serves on the college's National Gifts Program Committee.

Galen earned master's degrees in architecture and civil and urban engineering from the University of Pennsylvania in 1984. He was a Henry Luce Foundation research fellow at Tokyo University in 1982 and 1983 and received his bachelor's degree in physics from Haverford College in 1978.

Veronica W. Hackett
New York, New York

Veronica Hackett is the managing partner of the Clarett Group, a New York–based real estate company that develops mixed-use properties in urban areas. During her career, Hackett has developed over 13 million square feet (1.2 million m²) of real estate in New York and worldwide. Clarett Capital, formed with Prudential Real Estate Investors, currently has active development projects in New York, Los Angeles, and Washington, D.C., ranging in size from 150,000 to 1 million square feet (14,000 to 93,000 m²).

In addition to her work as a private sector developer, Hackett has been a corporate real estate executive in the United States and Europe, a real estate pension fund asset manager, a real estate lender, a Wall Street financial analyst, and a CIA economic analyst. She is a trustee of ULI and serves on the board of directors of the Real Estate Board of New York, the New York University Real Estate Institute, and the New York Building Congress. Hackett received her master's degree in finance from New York University and a bachelor's degree in history and economics from the College of Notre Dame of Maryland.

James D. Motta
Fort Lauderdale, Florida

James Motta is president of Starwood Land Company, LLC, a subsidiary of Starwood Capital Group, overseeing the development of the company's residential and resort investments in the eastern United States and the Caribbean. Prior to joining Starwood, Motta was president of the Motta Group, a Florida-based development company specializing in resort and residential communities. Previously, he served as president and CEO of St. Joe/Arvida Company, the residential real estate development and services arm of the St. Joe Company, and of St. Joe/Arvida's predecessor company, Arvida Company.

A graduate of the University of Florida, Motta is an active member of ULI, serving on its Recreational Development Council and on the executive committee of ULI's Southeast Florida District Council. Motta currently serves on the board of CentraCore Properties Trust, a New York Stock Exchange–listed company.

William B. Renner, Jr.
Fort Lauderdale, Florida

William Renner is a principal of EDSA, an international planning, landscape architecture, and urban design firm based in Florida. His concentration has been on urban, mixed-use projects and new community planning in the United States and abroad. Current projects include a resort community in Virginia, a new town in Tunisia, the redevelopment of Virginia Key near Miami, and a design for a new urban district of Abu Dhabi in the United Arab Emirates.

Renner received a master's degree in landscape architecture from Harvard University and a bachelor's degree from Bowdoin College. He has been with EDSA since 1986 and serves on its board of directors. He is active in ULI as a contributing author on publications, a member of special task forces on density and greenfield development, advisory panels, and on the executive committee of the South Florida District Council. He has lectured at Harvard University and at conferences for ULI, the American Planning Association, and the National Association of Home Builders.

Frank Ricks
Memphis, Tennessee

Frank Ricks is a founder and the managing principal of Looney Ricks Kiss (LRK), an architecture, interior design, planning, and environmental design research firm with a national staff that employs more than 200.

With a focus on urban renewal and redevelopment, Ricks has led his firm's involvement in projects like Harbor Town (Memphis, Tennessee), Baldwin Park (Orlando, Florida), WaterColor (Seagrove Beach, Florida), and the Memphis Ballpark District, all of which have won ULI Awards for Excellence. The Memphis Ballpark District, a 20-acre mixed-use development, also received the Congress for the New Urbanism's 2003 Charter Award.

Ricks is a past president of the Memphis chapter of the American Institute of Architects and a member of the Congress for the New Urbanism, Lambda Alpha International, and ULI. At ULI, he serves on the Mixed-Use Development Council, has participated on Advisory Services panels, and is a frequent meeting speaker and panelist. His professional degree is from the University of Memphis.

Robert Weekley
Los Angeles, California

Robert Weekley is a partner and a member of the executive committee of Lowe Enterprises, a privately held, multibillion-dollar, national real estate development, investment, asset management, and hospitality company. He has been with the firm for more than 25 years, with responsibility for strategy and implementation for a diverse range of real estate products representing more than $1 billion of activity throughout the United States.

Before joining Lowe, Weekley was founder and president of American Western Communities, a southern California residential developer emphasizing innovative multifamily for-sale and rental projects.

A graduate of Southern Methodist University and Harvard Business School, Weekley is involved in a variety of real estate industry, political, educational, and philanthropic endeavors and organizations.

Europe Jury

Andrea Amadesi, Jury Chair
Milan, Italy

Andrea Amadesi is the managing director of IXIS AEW Italy, a subsidiary of Caisse National des Caisses d'Epargne–Paris. Prior to joining IXIS AEW, he worked in investment banking in Paris and Milan, holding a variety of management positions and specializing in asset management and real estate investment. From 1989 to 1992, Amadesi was employed by Sotheby's as managing director of Italian operations. He was also the founder of the Milan Modern and Contemporary Art Fair.

Amadesi holds a degree in economics and commerce from the Bocconi University of Milan. He is a trustee of ULI, a governor of the ULI Foundation, and served as chairman of ULI Europe from 2002 to 2005.

Jan A. de Kreij
Utrecht, The Netherlands

Jan de Kreij is CEO of Corio NV, a Euronext-listed company in the Netherlands focused on European retail investments. Before joining Corio NV, he was CEO of Rodamco NV, a global real estate investor based in Rotterdam. And before that, he headed Royal Dutch Shell Oil Company's pension fund, which, under his leadership, became one of the largest investors in real estate in the United States and Europe in the 1980s.

As a former chair of ULI's European Policy and Practice Committee and the ULI Europe awards jury, and now as chair of ULI Europe, de Kreij is interested in sharing experiences with his U.S. counterparts. He currently holds a number of board positions in real estate and financial investment companies.

Ayse Hasol Erktin
Istanbul, Turkey

Ayse Hasol Erktin is a partner at HAS Architects, Ltd., a leading Turkish design/build firm, where she has worked for more than 15 years, designing and coordinating various housing, office, health care, and hospitality projects. Notable projects include the five-star Swissôtel Grand Hotel Efes and the 85,000-square-meter (914,932 sf) Soyak Center. Under her leadership, HAS formed project-based associations with Skidmore, Owings & Merrill in 1993, REES Associates, Inc., in 1999, NBBJ in 2003, and Pei, Cobb, Freed & Partners in 2005.

A graduate of Harvard University's Graduate School of Design, Erktin received a master's degree in business administration from Bogazici University and a bachelor's degree in architecture from Istanbul Technical University. She is an executive committee member of the ULI Turkey Council and has served as president of the Istanbul Project Management Association and vice president of the Harvard Alumni Club of Turkey. In her writing and speaking, Erktin focuses on the management of creativity and the value of design.

Anne T. Kavanagh
London, United Kingdom

Anne Kavanagh joined Cambridge Place Investment Management (CPIM), LLP, in 2006 as senior portfolio manager for real estate in Europe and as a member of CPIM's real estate investment and real estate asset review committees. Previously, she was an international director at Jones Lang LaSalle (JLL), where she led the team that advised JLL on the acquisition of its initial European portfolio. Since 2000, she has specialized in working with clients on cross-border transactions in Europe; she was an operating executive of JLL's European Capital Markets, which transacted over €15 billion (US$19 billion) per annum in the last five years. From 2003 to 2005, she served on the board of Asset Management & Accounting Services, Ltd., a business managing 10 million square meters (108 million sf) of real estate across all sectors.

From 1993 to 1999, Kavanagh led the London West End capital markets advisory team for JLL's predecessor firm, Jones Lang Wootton, which she joined in 1983. She holds a bachelor of science degree with honors in urban estate management from Nottingham Trent University and is a member of the Royal Institution of Chartered Surveyors.

Lee A. Polisano
London, United Kingdom

Lee Polisano is president of Kohn Pedersen Fox Associates' (KPF) international architecture practice group and founding partner of KPF's London studio. Under his direction, the firm's work focuses on response to context, awareness of the civic obligation of buildings, respect for the environment, and the importance of technology.

Polisano is responsible for many notable projects across Europe, including Heron Tower, London's first built-to-suit multitenant office building, and the Bishopsgate Tower, the tallest building in London's central business district. He is also directing urban planning and regeneration projects in Paris, Milan, and Amsterdam.

He holds degrees from LaSalle College in Philadelphia (B.A.) and Virginia Polytechnic Institute (M.Arch.) and was honored by the latter as the first recipient of VPI's Outstanding Professional Accomplishment Award. He is a Fellow of the American Institute of Architects, a member of the Royal Institute of British Architects, and a member of the Architektenkammer Berlin. He is a former cochair of ULI Europe's Office and Mixed-Use Council.

Asia Pacific Jury

Akio Makiyama, Jury Chair
Tokyo, Japan

Akio Makiyama is chairman of the Forum for Urban Development in Tokyo, which he founded in 1984. The purpose of the forum is to organize large-scale, public/private development, and it has launched more than 20 projects globally, encompassing the domains of business, politics, and culture. Currently, Makiyama is working to establish a new institute on global governance, which is tentatively named the Forum and Institute for Global Crisis Simulation Study (GLOCS-FORUM).

Makiyama graduated from Keio University's faculty of engineering in 1964. While a student, he organized his first cultural project—the All Japanese Student Mandolin Orchestra Society. Working for Mitsui & Company, Makiyama produced several projects at the 1970 Osaka World Expo and at the 1975 World Ocean Expo in Okinawa.

In 1977, he stood for national election as a New Liberal Club member, for which he served as the policy maker for foreign affairs and urban development. Makiyama organized and chaired the ULI Japan Council, securing the participation of key Japanese companies and public organizations. He has been a governor of the ULI Foundation since 2001.

Ivana Benda
Shanghai, China

Ivana Benda is a partner and design director of Allied Architects International (AAI), Inc., a design firm of more than 50 professionals licensed in Europe, North America, and China focused on the China market. AAI's senior management team has completed more than 150 projects in China.

A graduate of the Czech University of Technology, from which she received a master's degree in architecture, Benda is now enrolled in doctoral degree studies. She is a member of the Ontario Association of Architects and the Royal Architectural Institute of Canada. Before joining AAI, she was a senior associate, principal, coordinator, and design director in many international firms, such as B+H Architects International, Inc.

Benda has over 25 years of experience in all fields of the architectural profession. Although her design approach and basic understanding derive from her European education and background, most of her significant professional experience has been in North America and in China, where she began working in 1991. She joined ULI in 2002 to promote the practice of sustainable land development and architecture in Asia.

Sean Chuan-Sheng Chiao
Hong Kong

Sean Chiao is an urban designer and architect with extensive experience in the United States and Asia. He is the regional director of EDAW's Asia practice and serves on the board of EDAW, Inc.

As a pioneer of EDAW's collaborative approach and ethos in Asia, Chiao has directed multidisciplinary teams on projects ranging in scale and scope from master planning new communities to the visioning of new urban developments and major urban revitalization projects, as well as the design of major public open spaces. He has worked at both regional and local scales to formulate policies and strategies for city development and implementation, and at a neighborhood scale with community groups on the development of design briefs and guidelines. He has a proven track record in urban design and master planning for major public and private institutions and in fostering the management and implementation skills necessary to translate vision into reality.

Chiao earned a master's degree in architecture in urban design from Harvard University and a master's degree in architecture from the University of California at Berkeley.

Silas Chiow
Shanghai, China

Silas Chiow, AIA, serves as director of business development for the Greater China region at Skidmore, Owings and Merrill (SOM) in Shanghai. He is responsible for spearheading SOM's business strategies in Greater China and facilitating its architecture and planning projects throughout Asia.

Chiow began his career at SOM's New York office in 1987 and discovered his passion for the New York high rise while working on such notable projects as 180 Allyn Street, 320 Park Avenue, and the Wall Street Financial Center. In 1992, he won first prize at the Yokohama International Urban Design Competition and was invited to work in Nikken Sekkei's Tokyo office. There Chiow worked on major civic projects such as the Tokyo Government Center at Saitama, in addition to commercial projects in Tokyo and Singapore.

In 1995, Chiow joined SOM's San Francisco office, with the mission of providing leadership for the firm's China initiatives. In his 21-year career as an architect, urban planner, and project manager, he has gained experience and expertise in many development products, including hospitality, retail, mixed use, residential, convention centers, institutions, multifamily housing, and hotels.

Peter Verwer
Sydney, Australia

Peter Verwer is chief executive of the Property Council of Australia, the nation's leading advocate for investment property interests. The Property Council is an organization with more than 2,000 member companies and individuals in the commercial real estate industry. It employs 80 people, and its budget exceeds AU$18 million (US$13.5 million). In addition to its core business of advocacy and public affairs, the Property Council operates educational programs, conducts research, publishes, and offers networking services.

Verwer's current priorities are tax reform, economic growth, and regulatory reform. He is a member of many public and private sector organizations. He is a graduate of Sydney University, where he studied philosophy.

Yasuhiko Watanabe
Tokyo, Japan

Yasuhiko Watanabe is a senior adviser at Mitsubishi Estate Company (MEC), Ltd., one of the largest real estate companies in Japan. He currently provides direct counsel to MEC's entire commercial real estate business, which includes the development, leasing, and management of over 4 million square meters (43 million sf) of office and retail space throughout Japan.

Since he joined the company in 2000, he has played an integral role in MEC's large-scale reform of Marunouchi, Tokyo's premier business district. Prior to joining MEC, Watanabe spent 36 years with the Bank of Tokyo–Mitsubishi, Ltd., where he was responsible for international planning and was general manager of the Kyoto and Nagoya regions.

Watanabe holds a bachelor's degree in economics from Keio University and a master's degree from the Wharton School of Business at the University of Pennsylvania. He serves as council chair of ULI Japan, as vice chairman of the Japan Facility Management Promotion Association, and as a director of the Japan Building Owners and Managers Association.

Stephany Naifen Yu
Shanghai, China

Stephany Yu is founder and chairman of Shanghai Luting Group, Ltd., a real estate development enterprise focused on mixed-use, residential, and other projects in China. Shanghai Luting has delivered more than 100,000 square meters (1.1 million sf) per year to Shanghai's urban and suburban markets for the past three years. Yu received a master's degree in economics from Fudan University in Shanghai and worked and studied in the United States from 1990 to 1994.

2005 ULI GLOBAL AWARDS FOR EXCELLENCE

The ULI Global Awards for Excellence recognize projects that provide the best cross-regional lessons in land use practices. Up to five global winners may be named each year—chosen from among the year's 20 winners in the Americas, Europe, and Asia Pacific—by a select jury of international members.

In 2005, the awards' inaugural year, three global winners were announced at the ULI Fall Meeting in Los Angeles, November 4. In 2006, up to five global award winners will be announced at the Fall Meeting in Denver, October 20.

As three renowned and informed juries already have chosen winners that meet ULI criteria for awards, the Global Awards Jury uses slightly different and additional criteria in identifying projects that:

- Establish innovative concepts or standards for development that can be emulated around the world;
- Show strong urban design qualities;
- Respond to the context of the surrounding environment;
- Demonstrate awareness of issues contributing to a universally desirable configuration of development, such as: sustainable development, environmental responsibility, pedestrian-friendly design, smart growth practices, and development around transit; and
- Demonstrate relevance to the present and future needs of the community in which they are located.

The Global Awards Jury

The chairman of ULI appoints the jury, composed of five distinguished land use development and design experts, led by the chair of ULI's Policy and Practice Committee, and represented by the chairs of the three regional awards juries (or a designate) and an at-large jury member chosen by the chairman of ULI. In 2005, jury members were:

Todd Mansfield, Jury Chair, *chief executive officer, Crosland, Inc., Charlotte, North Carolina*

Sean Chuan-Sheng Chiao, *regional director, principal, EDAW Urban Design, Ltd., Hong Kong*

Gerald Hines, *chairman and owner, Hines, Houston, Texas*

Jan de Kreij, *chief executive officer, Corio NV, Utrecht, The Netherlands*

Diana Permar, *president, Permar, Inc., Charleston, South Carolina*

Winners of 2005 ULI Global Awards for Excellence

Hangzhou Waterfront, Hangzhou, People's Republic of China

Owner/Developer: Hangzhou Hubin Commerce & Tourism Company, Ltd.

Jury Statement

The city of Hangzhou has put West Lake—storied in Chinese poetry and legend—on the international map through a large-scale public improvement of its scenic waterfront. The lively mixed-use development and pedestrian-oriented spaces have given Hangzhou's citizens a new amenity that is environmentally sensitive and encourages new high-quality development.

Marunouchi Building, Tokyo, Japan

Owner/Developer: Mitsubishi Estate Company, Ltd.

Jury Statement

As Japan's first modern office building, the Marunouchi Building was a landmark in 1923. Today, with the construction within the original footprint of a 31-story tower atop a five-story podium, the building resumes its landmark status, setting a new high standard for historic preservation, upgrading the character and value of its central Tokyo neighborhood, attracting new nightlife and weekend activity, and providing a model for the revitalization of CBDs everywhere.

Millennium Park, Chicago, Illinois

Owners/Developers: City of Chicago; Millennium Park, Inc; and U.S. Equities Realty

Jury Statement

Millennium Park offers a new model for creating a park through public/private partnerships of city agencies, private developers, artists, and individual donors and philanthropies. Developed in the air rights above rail yards, the project—24.5 acres (9.9 ha) of open space, architecturally significant buildings, and outstanding artworks atop below-grade parking—has revitalized land values along South Michigan Avenue and created a world-class park in a city whose motto is Urbs in Horto (City in a Garden).